The
Seven
Pillories
of Wisdom

Wisdom has built herself a house,
she has erected her seven pillars.
—Proverbs 9:1 (Jerusalem Bible)

The Seven Pillories of Wisdom

by David R. Hall

PEETERS

MERCER

ISBN 0-86554-369-0

The paper used in this publication meets
the minimum requirements of American National Standard
for Information Sciences—Permanence of Paper
for Printed Library Materials, ANSI Z39.48-1984.

Library of Congress Cataloging-in-Publication Data
Hall, David R.
   The seven pillories of wisdom / by David R. Hall
   viii + 134pp. 6 × 9in. (15 × 23cm.)
   Includes bibliographical references.
   Includes index.
   ISBN 0-86554-369-0 (alk. paper)
   1. Bible. N.T.—Criticism, interpretation, etc.—History—19th century.
2. Bible. N.T.—Criticism, interpretation, etc.—History—20th century.
3. Bible. N.T.—Hermeneutics. I. Title. II. Title: 7 pillories of wisdom.
BS2350.H28   1990   90-35442
220.6'01—dc20   CIP

Contents

Introduction

This book is an argument about arguments. I propose to examine seven arguments that have been used from time to time by New Testament scholars during the last century and a half. Many theories about the New Testament have been built on the foundation of these arguments. It is therefore important to raise the question of their validity; for if the foundation of a building is unsound, the superstructure will also be unsound.

There is a natural tendency to take foundations on trust. Most of us have never seen the foundations of the house we live in. We repair the walls and roof and rearrange the furniture, but presuppose the foundations. The only way we can tell whether or not the foundations are sound is by looking for cracks in the superstructure.

In the case of a house, this is understandable. The foundations of a house are normally invisible and inaccessible. This is not the case, however, with the structures of biblical criticism. The modern student of the Bible is confronted with a variety of approaches to the Bible, ranging from the extreme conservative to the extreme radical, each of which is based upon foundations laid down many years ago. These foundations are documented and accessible. The problem is that most students of the Bible do not have the time to dig into the foundations of the various approaches. We are tempted to adopt that approach to the Bible whose visible structure appeals to us, and to forget that, if we adopt a theology someone else has constructed without testing the foundation, we do so at our peril.

In his contribution to *Essays and Reviews* in 1860 Benjamin Jowett drew a contrast between theologians and scholars in other disciplines. Natural scientists, he believed, felt it to be useless to build on assumptions; historians looked with suspicion on a priori ideas of what ought to have been; mathematicians, when a step was wrong, pulled the house down until they reached the point at which the error was discovered. But in theology Jowett discerned a different attitude. There was a tendency, he discovered, to conceal the unsoundness of the foundation under the fairness and loftiness of the superstructure. It was thought safer to allow arguments to stand which, although fallacious, were on the right side, than to point out their defects. In this way, Jowett declared, "many principles have imperceptibly grown up which have overridden facts."[1]

Jowett had in mind the nineteenth-century opposition to biblical criticism. He was insisting that our understanding of the inspiration of the Bible must be based, not on dogma, but on examination of the Bible itself, as illuminated by "all well-ascertained facts of history or of science." In one sense the battle Jowett fought has already been won. But in another sense, as new orthodoxies take the place of the old, each generation has to fight the battle afresh. Each generation has to ask how far the current orthodoxy is based on well-ascertained facts of history or of science, and how far it is building on assumptions.

During the last hundred years there has evolved a way of thinking about the New Testament that may be called, for want of a better term, modern critical orthodoxy. Those scholars who accept the presuppositions of modern critical orthodoxy live in a kind of intellectual house whose foundations were laid many years ago by such men as David Friedrich Strauss, Ferdinand Christian Baur, and William Wrede. The detailed opinions of these men have been modified by later generations, but their general approach has been of more lasting influence. Many of the arguments I shall be examining were pioneered by these men, and then taken over and presupposed by those who followed them. I shall therefore feel free, when questioning the validity of these arguments, to refer to their past history as well as to their current use.

This will involve reference to some scholarly techniques, such as form criticism, and to some scholars, such as Rudolf Bultmann, whose heyday was an earlier generation. At first sight this might seem like flogging a dead horse. New Testament scholarship, some would say, has moved on from the days of form criticism to newer and more exciting fields of study. But such a statement is at best a half-truth. Certainly there are modern scholars who reject completely the form-critical method. But most scholars, so far as I can see, while recognizing the limitations of form criticism in point of detail, have not rejected the presuppositions on which that method rests. So long as this is the case, critical examination of those presuppositions will always be necessary.

The tone of this book is mainly—but I hope not entirely—negative. For this I make no apology, but echo the words of A. E. Housman: "I have spent most of my time finding faults because finding faults, if they are real and not imaginary, is the most useful sort of criticism."[2]

---

[1]Benjamin Jowett, "On the Interpretation of Scripture," in *Essays and Reviews,* ed. J. Parker (London: Longmans, 1860) 414.

[2]Alfred Edward Housman, *Selected Prose* (Cambridge: Cambridge University Press, 1961) xii.

The Argument from Up-to-Dateness

1

"Anything that anybody talks about, and says there's a good deal in it, extends itself indefinitely like a vista in a nightmare." —Father Brown[1]

The argument from up-to-dateness assumes that a modern idea should be preferred to an ancient one simply because it is modern. This way of thinking has a long pedigree, going back at least to the Athenians of St. Paul's day who "liked to spend all their time telling and hearing the latest new thing."[2] But the pressure to be up-to-date is stronger now than it has ever been. This is partly a consequence of the pace of change and the explosion of knowledge in the twentieth century; but it is also a pathological condition—a state of mind artificially fostered by modern advertising techniques. Vance Packard has described the theory behind this:

> By the mid-fifties merchandisers of many different products were being urged by psychological counsellors to become "merchants of discontent." One ad executive exclaimed with fervor: "what makes this country great is the creation of wants and desires, the creation of dissatisfaction with the old and outmoded."[3]

The results of this pressure can be seen all around us. In many Western societies the stores no longer sell "clothes," they sell "fashions." In the days when they sold clothes, the garments were designed to last for many years. But fashions change from year to year and from season to season.

Fashions influence what people believe as well as what they wear. G. K. Chesterton's character, Lord Beaumont of Foxwood, was a man whose beliefs were

---

[1] Gilbert Keith Chesterton, *The Incredulity of Father Brown* (Harmondsworth, England: Penguin Books, 1958) 71.

[2] The Acts of the Apostles 17:21 (Today's English Version alias Good News Bible).

[3] Vance Packard, *The Hidden Persuaders* (London: Penguin Books, 1960) 24.

determined by fashion. He thought anything new must be an advance. If you went
to him and proposed to eat your grandmother, he would agree with you, so long
as you put it on hygienic and public grounds, as a cheap alternative to cremation.
So long as you progressed fast enough, he did not mind whether you were progressing to the stars or to the devil.[4]

Karl Popper has called this way of thinking "progressivism." When Popper
was a young man in Vienna, this was the attitude towards music of Schönberg and
his circle. They started as disciples of Wagner, but then were concerned to
supersede Wagner, to remain ahead of everyone else, and even to supersede themselves. Yet Popper observed that those great artists who were blessed with the gift
of originality, such as Bach, Mozart, and Schubert, never tried to be leaders of
fashion or to create a new "style" in music. He was therefore skeptical of fashion
following in other fields:

> Even in philosophy one hears of a new style of philosophizing, or of a "Phi-
> losophy in a New Key"—as if it were the key that mattered rather than the
> tune played, and as if it mattered whether the key was old or new.[5]

For most people the desire to be up-to-date takes a more modest form than
progressivism. Shoppers who cannot afford a new wardrobe every year prefer to
see which fashions become popular before investing their money. They believe in
what may be called moderate up-to-dateness—styles that are sufficiently new to
be fashionable and sufficiently old to be respectable.

In study of the New Testament moderate up-to-dateness means adopting those
opinions that, in the course of the twentieth century, have acquired a kind of orthodox status. People talk of a "consensus of modern scholarship" (in Latin, *quod
nuper, quod ubique*), or of "the assured results of modern criticism." While it is
recognized that these assured results may be revised by scholars in the future, the
orthodoxy of the present is still felt to be, at the very least, an improvement on the
orthodoxies of the past—of the primitive, prescientific days of the early church,
the Dark Ages, and the Reformation.

In all areas of life—and study of the New Testament is no exception—there
is a psychological pressure to accept *current* orthodoxy. The nature of this pressure has been analyzed by Peter Berger. We are social beings and most of what
we "know" is taken on the authority of others. If our knowledge is shared by others around us we feel confident. If our knowledge is not socially shared it becomes
difficult to believe, not only for others, but also for ourselves. In Berger's words,

---

[4]Gilbert Keith Chesterton, *The Club of Queer Trades* (Beaconsfield, England: Darwen Finlayson, 1960) 43.

[5]Karl Raimund Popper, *Unended Quest* (London: Collins, 1976) 71-72.

"At best, a minority viewpoint is forced to be defensive. At worst, it ceases to be plausible to anyone."[6]

It follows from this that, whether or not the results of modern criticism are "assured" in any objective sense, accepting them brings a feeling of assurance to our minds. Even if we are wrong, we are wrong in good company. As A. E. Housman put it, "the disciple resorts to the teacher, and the request he makes of him is not *tell me how to get rid of error,* but *tell me how to get rid of doubt.*"[7]

In this chapter I wish to examine two of the arguments for preferring the theories of the twentieth century to those of earlier centuries. One of these arguments appeals to the dogma of evolutionism. The other alleges that twentieth-century thought is scientific in a way in which the thought of earlier centuries was not. I shall conclude by contrasting the shortsighted and the longsighted approaches to scholarship.

The Dogma of Evolutionism

Evolutionism is not the scientific theory of Evolution, but the philosophical theory that human thought is continually progressing so that the ideas of today are necessarily an improvement on the ideas of yesterday. The scholars of tomorrow will make yet further improvements; but in doing so they will take today's ideas as their starting point, just as we are now building on the foundation laid by those who lived before us. In this way scholarship is steadily advancing. Each generation adds a storey to the skyscraper of knowledge as it reaches to the sky. In the words of James Russell Lowell,

New occasions teach new duties,
Time makes ancient good uncouth;
They must upward still and onward
Who would keep abreast of truth.[8]

I propose to indicate some of the limitations of the evolutionist approach, and then to suggest some alternative models for understanding the history of human thought.

The limitations of evolutionism. The "upward still and onward" approach makes sense in those fields of study that depend on technical know-how. No one

---

[6]Peter L. Berger, *A Rumor of Angels* (New York: Doubleday, 1969) 8.

[7]Alfred Edward Housman, *The Confines of Criticism* (Cambridge: Cambridge University Press, 1969) 40.

[8]James Russell Lowell, "The Present Crisis" (1845) as excerpted in the *Methodist Hymn Book* (London: Methodist Conference Office, 1933) hymn 898.

would deny that our capacity to build bridges across rivers or to manufacture computers is greater now than it has ever been. But R. G. Collingwood has made the point that progress often goes hand in hand with decline. The invention of firearms led to the decline of archery; the development of printing led to the decline of the manuscript book. The present is built upon the past, and in that sense history is a progress. But none of the phases through which it moves is better or worse than any other.[9]

Collingwood illustrated this from architecture. Gothic buildings were definitely an improvement on Norman buildings from an engineering point of view; but that did not make them better as works of art. The connoisseur of architecture, in Collingwood's view, is merely confessing his own personal limitations if he says he likes Gothic for its slenderness and dislikes Norman for its fatness. He ought to enjoy the spire of Salisbury Cathedral because it soars; he ought to enjoy Durham Cathedral because it does not soar but stands square and stout on its rock.[10]

In study of the New Testament it is important to ask whether the views of modern scholars, where they differ from the views of earlier scholars, are based on superior technical know-how or simply on a change in attitudes and presuppositions. If the latter is the case, we should not assume that on any particular issue scholarship is automatically moving "upward still and onward." Rather, like a car travelling from coast to coast, its onward movement is likely to be both upward and downward in equal proportions.

In his essay "The Funeral of a Great Myth," C. S. Lewis pronounced a funeral oration over what he called "the great myth of the nineteenth and early twentieth century"—the myth of Evolutionism. Lewis's objection was that, unlike the scientific theory of evolution (which was a theory about *changes*), the myth of Evolutionism was concerned with *improvements*. According to Professor J. B. S. Haldane, progress was not the rule in evolution but the exception; for every case of progress there were ten cases of degeneration. But Lewis observed that the myth simply expurgated the ten cases of degeneration. The word "evolution" conjured up a picture of things moving "onwards and upwards" and of nothing else.[11]

If Lewis was right, evolutionary ideas have only a limited relevance to the history of scholarship. The chances of the latest development being an improvement on the ideas it has superseded are, on Haldane's reckoning, ten-to-one against.

We should bear this in mind when reading any book that deals with the historical development of New Testament scholarship. One of the best of such books

---

[9]Robin George Collingwood, *Essays in the Philosophy of History* (Austin: University of Texas Press, 1965) 81-86.

[10]Ibid,. 109-11.

[11]Clive Staples Lewis, *Christian Reflections* (London: Collins, 1981) 110-23.

is W. G. Kümmel's *The New Testament: The History of the Investigation of Its Problems,* a comprehensive survey of a wide range of scholars. However, in his preface Kümmel writes that he has deliberately limited the scope of his book to "the lines of inquiry and the methods which have proved to be of permanent significance or to anticipate future developments." The two latter ideas seem to be linked—the "permanent significance" of an earlier scholar's line of inquiry being dependent on whether or not it has led to "future developments" in the next generation. In the case of present-day research it is the scholars of the future who will determine, by developing or failing to develop it, whether or not it is permanently significant. In Kümmel's words, "whether a new line of inquiry was permanently important and was later to prove fruitful cannot easily be determined for the period of research to which we ourselves belong." He therefore limits himself to scholars of the past, since of them he knows whose research has "proved fruitful" in the sense of being developed by other scholars, and can thus assess whose research has been of "permanent significance."[12]

This method of assessment is appropriate to any study that views New Testament research as a historical or sociological phenomenon. Scholars in the nineteenth and twentieth centuries have in fact pursued certain lines of inquiry more than others, and the criterion of fruitfulness is helpful to theological genealogists who wish to trace the pedigree of the presuppositions of modern scholarship. It is important, however, not to equate the fruitfulness of a line of research (defined in terms of its popularity with the next generation of researchers) with its validity. The fact that a line of inquiry begun by Scholar A was developed by a hundred scholars in the next generation does not make that line of inquiry more valid than that of Scholar B whose work is almost forgotten. Scholar A's work was certainly fruitful in the propagation of doctoral theses, but *not necessarily* in the propagation of truth.

In his book *The Use of Lateral Thinking* Edward de Bono contrasts two types of thought process. What he calls "vertical thinking" is the logical working out of a dominant idea. He compares it to the continued excavation of an old hole because it is easier to go on digging in the same place than to start a new hole. The first principle of what he calls "lateral thinking" is to realize that dominant ideas can be an obstacle rather than an asset. In other words, there is an element of discontinuity in the progress of human thought.[13]

This element of discontinuity is generally recognized so far as the origins of modern critical orthodoxy are concerned. Kümmel describes the discussion of the

---

[12]Werner Georg Kümmel, *The New Testament: The History of the Investigation of Its Problems,* trans. S. McLean Gilmour and Howard Clark Kee (London: SCM Press; Nashville/New York: Abingdon Press, 1972) 7.

[13]Edward de Bono, *The Use of Lateral Thinking* (London: Penguin Books, 1971) 22.

New Testament prior to the eighteenth century as "the prehistory of New Testament scholarship." What began with the Enlightenment was something new: a "scientific" view of the New Testament which considered it "without dogmatic or creedal bias."[14] In de Bono's terms, modern critical study of the New Testament started to dig a new hole. But once excavation has started, should work on the same hole progress indefinitely? How often do new holes need to be dug?

In the years since Kümmel's book was first published many scholars have attempted to dig a new hole by ignoring historical problems and concentrating on the New Testament as literature. I shall discuss this in more detail later. All I wish to say at this point is that, so far as I can see, this new approach has supplemented the old approach but has not superseded it. The dominant ideas of modern critical orthodoxy are still dominant; and so long as this is the case the question of their validity must continue to be raised.

We need to ask the question, What paths did New Testament scholars follow in the nineteenth and twentieth centuries? But the more important question is, Were the scholars right to follow those paths? The fact that a scholar has disciples who develop his or her ideas does not tell us anything about whether or not those ideas are sound, as Humphrey Palmer has pointed out:

> Bultmann, surveying in 1962 the progress of the movement he has helped to found, claimed that "the soundness of Form Criticism has been demonstrated in recent years, since it has served, and still continues to serve, as the presupposition of further research." Unfortunately, it is quite possible for research along a certain line to be carried on even though the presuppositions on which it is based are in fact *un*sound.[15]

In other words, the theory of natural selection and the survival of the fittest does not necessarily apply in the field of New Testament research.

Alternatives to evolutionism. There are several alternatives to the evolutionist model for interpreting the history of human thought. One is the model of the pendulum—oscillation rather than progression. This is the model implied in A. E. Housman's dictum: "error, if allowed to run its course, secures its own downfall, and is sooner or later overthrown, not by the truth, but by error of an opposite kind."[16] In the opinion of Carl Braaten this model applies to a great deal of modern scholarship. He sees the pendulum swing back and forth, particularly in German theology, as school after school constructs its theological position on one principle: "The

---

[14]Kümmel, *The New Testament,* 13.

[15]Humphrey Palmer, *The Logic of Gospel Criticism* (London: Macmillan; New York: St. Martin's Press, 1968) 175.

[16]Alfred Edward Housman, *M. Manilii Astronomicon I* (Cambridge: Cambridge University Press, 1937) xliii.

ultimatum 'either/or' is more exhilarating than the balanced 'both/and.' Disciples of these schools languish under the tyranny of a single principle.''[17]

Stephen Neill gave an example of the oscillation process in his survey of the criticism of the Fourth Gospel in the period 1861–1961. Traditionally John was regarded as the most reliable of the four gospels, written by the apostle himself. Radical criticism of the mid-nineteenth century swung to an opposite extreme, and denied to the gospel any historical value, or any connection with the apostle. The last quarter of the nineteenth century saw a swing back to a more conservative position. Then came, at the turn of the century, what Neill called ''a violent reaction against a reaction,'' in which six scholars at about the same time claimed that John's gospel was not history but a translation of the gospel into the terms of Greek philosophy. This was followed by a counterreaction. The Jewish element in the gospel was emphasized once again. C. F. Burney even claimed that John was originally written in Aramaic, the mother tongue of Jesus. And so the debate goes on, with some scholars oscillating towards a Jewish origin for the gospel, some towards a Greek origin, and others trying to maintain equilibrium in the center.[18]

Perhaps we should revise Lowell's poem in the light of the pendulum model:

Fashions new are fashions ancient,
Time revives the ancient good;
They must to-and-fro and sideways
Who are toujours à la mode.

The best model for New Testament scholarship is, in my opinion, the boomerang. Suppose you spend a week's holiday at a tourist center. Every day you leave the center by a different route. Some routes take you to beautiful and exciting places. Others may take you to a dead end—a precipice or a railway terminus. But wherever your route has led you, you return each night to the center. The center is both the starting point and the destination for all the journeys that radiate from it.

For the student of the New Testament the New Testament is the center. A new route should not start at the end of the route followed by a previous scholar; nor should it swing in the opposite direction to that of a previous scholar. Every new route should start from the center, from that scholar's independent study of the New Testament itself. This was the model advocated by the great Cambridge scholar F. J. A. Hort who, when asked to recommend the best introduction to the

---

[17]Carl E. Braaten, *History and Hermeneutics,* New Directions in Theology Today 2 (Philadelphia: Westminster Press, 1966; London: Lutterworth Press, 1968) 51.

[18]Stephen Charles Neill, *The Interpretation of the New Testament 1861–1961,* corrected ed. (London, New York, and Toronto: Oxford University Press, 1966) 313-24.

Synoptic Problem, replied, "I should advise you to take your Greek Testament and get your own view of the facts first of all."[19]

According to Model A (the evolutionist model) scholarship is like a relay race: the source critic hands on the baton to the form critic, who hands it over to the redaction critic, and so on. In a relay race each changeover takes place at a further distance from the starting point. The danger with the relay-race approach to New Testament scholarship is that the later runners may be in touch with the starting point (the New Testament) only indirectly, through what is handed on to them by previous runners. Because they want to win the race, and uphold the honor of the school of interpretation in whose colors they are running, they may not have time to go back to the starting point to check whether or not they have received the correct baton.

According to Model B (the pendulum model) scholarship is like a three-day cricket match. The side scoring runs one day find themselves fielding the next day, with some broad-minded scholars acting as umpires in the middle. The fact that on one particular day one side is scoring runs does not mean they will win the match. Many matches end without a decision.

According to Model C (the boomerang model) scholarship is like a golf tournament, in which the players end each day at the place where they started. The aim of a player may sometimes be to follow the route of an earlier player and go further. It may sometimes be to swing in the opposite direction to that of an earlier player. But the main aim of any player is to get the ball in the hole. The very first player, if his or her sense of direction is good, is as likely to win as any of the others.

Scientific Method

The second common reason for preferring modern critical orthodoxy to traditional orthodoxy is the belief that the theories and methods of modern New Testament scholars are scientific, whereas the theories and methods of scholars of earlier centuries were not. In order to evaluate this belief, we must first ask the question, What do we mean by scientific method? and then ask whether modern New Testament scholars do in fact follow this method. The twentieth century has seen tremendous advances in scientific discovery; but that does not make every child of the twentieth century a scientist. If ducks can swim in water without getting wet, scholars can live in a scientific age without imbibing the scientific spirit. G. K. Clark has rightly said that "what claims to have the authority of science

---

[19]Fenton John Anthony Hort as quoted in Gordon Rupp, *Just Men* (London: Epworth Press, 1977) 161.

ought to be endorsed by the rigours of scientific proof, otherwise it is mere assertion couched in technical terms.''[20]

One possible approach to defining scientific method is that of Karl Popper. In his autobiography Popper described how he rebelled in his youth against the dogmatic attitude of Marx, Freud, Adler, and their followers:

> The encounter with Marxism . . . taught me the wisdom of the Socratic saying, ''I know that I do not know.'' It made me a fallibilist, and impressed on me the value of intellectual modesty. And it made me most conscious of the differences between dogmatic and critical thinking.[21]

Through the influence of Einstein, Popper came to believe that the scientific attitude was the critical attitude, which did not look for verifications but for crucial tests, tests that could *refute* the theory tested though they could never establish it.[22] However well a theory came through its time of testing, it could never be more than a working hypothesis. To Popper, one of the consequences of the Einsteinian revolution was ''the hypothetical character of all scientific theories.''[23]

If we accept an approach such as Popper's to scientific inquiry, it will have several implications for study of the New Testament.

Theories must be tested as rigorously as possible.

In Stephen Neill's judgment, theologians tended to be weak at two points where physical scientists were strong. The first was the ruthless spirit of self-criticism in which scientists tested their own work. The second was the rejection of hypotheses that had failed to stand up to the tests to which they had been subjected. What hindered progress in theology, according to Neill, was ''the persistence in currency of hypotheses in favour of which solid and satisfactory evidence has never been adduced.''[24]

The twentieth century has spawned a large number of hypotheses about the authorship and composition of the books of the New Testament. Those wishing to test these hypotheses are faced with two problems: lack of evidence and shortage of time.

So far as the evidence is concerned, we know very little about the life of the churches in the first century, and external evidence about the situations in which New Testament books were written is almost totally lacking. The testing of the-

---

[20]George Sidney Roberts Kitson Clark, *The Critical Historian* (London: Heinemann; New York: Basic Books, 1967) 21.

[21]Popper, *Unended Quest,* 36.

[22]Ibid., 38.

[23]Ibid., 81.

[24]Neill, *Interpretation,* 346.

ories of composition that is usually done is an internal testing—looking at the gospels and epistles and seeing whether they fit in with the theory. The more elastic the theory, the easier the fit.

The results of this procedure can be illustrated from J. A. T. Robinson's book *Redating the New Testament*. One day Robinson decided, as "little more than a theological joke," to see how far he could get with the hypothesis that the whole of the New Testament was written before A.D. 70. Soon the joke became a serious preoccupation, as he discovered how little hard evidence there was for the commonly accepted dating of most New Testament books. What seemed to be firm datings based on scientific evidence were revealed to rest on deductions from deductions. When Robinson questioned some of the inbuilt assumptions, the whole edifice looked insecure.[25] Typical of his findings was Austin Farrer's comment on the attempt to date the Apocalypse in relation to the Synoptic Gospels:

> The datings of all these books are like a line of tipsy revellers walking home arm-in-arm; each is kept in position by the others and none is firmly grounded. The whole series can lurch five years this way or that, and still not collide with a solid obstacle.[26]

Students of the "form" of the New Testament writings face the same problem as estimators of their dating. In Humphrey Palmer's judgment the form critics labored under a special limitation, that until gramophones were invented no instances of purely oral tradition could be preserved by which to regulate their theories of development. Their consequent reliance on distant analogies with Teutonic folklore made their work seem to Palmer unnecessarily skeptical.[27]

At first sight it might seem that a theory for which there is no external evidence is thereby weakened, but in practice it may be strengthened. The fact that it cannot be properly tested means that it cannot be properly refuted. Chris Morgan and David Langford quote the theory that eels can be generated spontaneously from hair from horses' tails. To generate spontaneous eels, you need only put a few hairs in water and wait. If you get no eels, you have performed the experiment wrongly. The authors comment that "the great advantage of theories like these is that they cannot be disproved."[28]

The problem of lack of evidence is often compounded by the problem of shortage of time. None of us has the time to examine the pros and cons of every

---

[25]John Arthur Thomas Robinson, *Redating the New Testament* (London: SCM Press, 1976) 1-10.

[26]Ibid., 343.

[27]Palmer, *Gospel Criticism*, 51.

[28]Chris Morgan and David Langford, *Facts and Fallacies* (Exeter: Webb and Bower, 1981) 15.

issue that confronts us. Ninety-nine percent of what any person believes is taken on trust from other people. G. K. Clark has pointed out how this affects the world of scholarship.

> It is not possible for scholars to reconsider and check all the evidence used by other scholars. If they felt called upon to do so the wheels of scholarship would grind to a halt. Scholars must in some matters take other people's work as a starting point, and when they do this they are like everyone else completely dependent on the integrity, accuracy, and critical capacity of the people whose work they use.[29]

In other words, a scholarly consensus is likely to consist largely of secondhand opinions. A. E. Housman, surveying the opinions about classical texts commonly accepted in his day, observed that "this planet is largely inhabited by parrots."[30]

This raises the possibility that a theory backed by many people may never have been properly tested. Its supporters may be relying on each other instead of testing each other. If we try to build a house with cards, we discover that two cards leaning on each other are both equally vulnerable. Their mutual support is of the kind described some years ago in a story in the *Reader's Digest*.

The story concerns a time-and-motion inspector on a visit to a factory. He was told that a man on the roof fired a gun at one o'clock every day to signal the end of the lunch break. The man knew when to fire the gun by checking the time on the clock outside the chemist's shop in the High Street. The inspector then went and asked the chemist how often his clock was checked. "Never," he replied. "It's always dead right by the one o'clock gun."[31]

Despite the problem of shortage of time, however, there is a long tradition in New Testament study of scholarly caution—of refusing to accept new theories unless the data are sufficient. An outstanding representative of this tradition was the nineteenth-century British scholar F. J. A. Hort, to whom Gordon Rupp paid tribute in his lecture "Hort and the Cambridge Tradition."[32]

One of Hort's characteristics was the passion for accurate detail. Armitage Robinson described how he never seemed to trust to memory: book after book came down from the shelves in the course of conversation; fact after fact was verified.[33] Hort declared himself unwilling to accept a "mere balancing of indecisive evidence" when there was fair reason to hope that a little more work would bring

---

[29]Clark, *Critical Historian*, 119.

[30]Housman, *Astronomicon*, xxxii.

[31]*Reader's Digest*, British edition, April 1982, 123.

[32]Rupp, *Just Men*, 151-66.

[33]Ibid., 157.

sufficiently decisive evidence to light. He was willing to sacrifice much grudged time "in order to make a trustworthy opinion possible." As a result, his published works were few, each the product of massive learning and research. He was amazed at his contemporary Adolf Harnack, who at the height of his career produced 455 writings in fourteen years: "His speed is to me a constant marvel, but it is a great snare to him. He never seems to have been taught to think three times before he speaks."[34]

The great Sherlock Holmes once remarked in conversation with another detective, "the temptation to form premature theories upon insufficient data is the bane of our profession."[35] Of the many parallels between the work of a detective and that of a New Testament scholar, this temptation is surely one.

It must be recognized that hypotheses are hypothetical.

Much modern criticism of the New Testament follows what is known as the inductive method. You put forward a new theory, and see how it works out in practice. There are obvious reasons for preferring the inductive to the deductive method. The deductive method has grave disadvantages. If the basis of my beliefs is dogma laid down by church councils or any other authority, then it is not possible for me to discuss my beliefs freely with anyone whose dogmas differ from mine. Scholarship, as it is generally thought of today, becomes impossible.

However, the inductive method also has its limitations. Let us suppose that, by taking a particular theory as a working hypothesis, an elaborate reconstruction of the process of composition of some part of the New Testament can be made which fits most or all of the known facts. This does not establish the truth of the theory. We know so little about the early church that almost any theory can be fitted to the facts, given enough ingenuity and imagination.

E. F. Schumacher has observed that a similar situation prevails in the instructional sciences such as physics and chemistry. You can prove that a certain set of instructions works; but you cannot prove that other instructions might not work equally well. The pre-Copernican instructions on how to calculate the movements inside the solar system, based on the theory that the sun moved round the earth, for a long time produced much more accurate results than the post-Copernican instructions.[36]

In the case of New Testament criticism the inductive method has special limitations. Study of the New Testament is largely concerned with questions of his-

---

[34]Ibid., 161.

[35]Arthur Conan Doyle, "The Valley of Fear," in *The Complete Sherlock Holmes Long Stories* (London: John Murray and Jonathan Cape, 1977) 424.

[36]Ernst Friedrich Schumacher, *A Guide for the Perplexed* (London: Sphere Books, 1978) 125.

tory, and the inductive methods of natural science cannot simply be taken over in the study of history. G. K. Clark has explained why this is so. Scientists are able to isolate the subject of their inquiry, and then to make repeated experiments upon it in controlled conditions. But in history it is difficult to isolate the factors at work and impossible to repeat experiments. There is therefore, in Clark's words, "a great gulf fixed between the results of historical and of scientific thought."[37]

The danger in following the inductive method in an area where it cannot be properly applied is obvious. Scholars can show that a particular hypothesis "works" in that the evidence can be interpreted to fit in with it. They are tempted to assume from this that the hypothesis has been demonstrated, and to use it as a presupposition for further research. If this happens, what began as induction can easily end up as deduction—building the ideas of the present day on the foundation of the unproved hypotheses of the past.

Hypotheses must never be upgraded to axioms through lapse of time.

When a theory has been proclaimed for a long time by influential people, there is a temptation to assume that the theory must be correct. In his survey of the interpretation of the New Testament between 1861 and 1961, Stephen Neill observed how, by constant reiteration, certain affirmations had come to be treated almost as axioms.[38] Among these "quasi-axioms" were the following.

(1) The theory that the early church made little distinction between words Jesus spoke during his ministry in Palestine, and words spoken in the name of Jesus by early Christian prophets. This theory, in Neill's opinion, ran contrary to all the evidence available.[39]

(2) The theory that there was a myth circulating in the ancient world, before the time of Christ, in which a heavenly redeemer came to earth, took human form, revealed himself to his disciples, and then returned to his heavenly home. For this myth in this form Neill could find no evidence at all.[40]

(3) The theory that there were Gentile churches in the cities of the Roman Empire that were almost independent of the church in Jerusalem, and that drew their picture of Jesus, not from the tradition of the apostles, but from their Gentile environment. For this theory also Neill could find no evidence, and he commented on the strange fact that, in one of the most distinguished books of this century on New Testament theology, the work of Rudolf Bultmann, thirty pages were devoted to the message and teaching of Jesus, and a hundred pages to the life and thought of Gentile communities that may never have existed.[41]

---

[37]Clark, *Critical Historian*, 22.

[38]Neill, *Interpretation*, 257.

[39]Ibid., 262.

[40]Ibid., 167-81.

[41]Ibid., 182.

Why, we may ask, are such quasi-axioms believed? One possible reason is that they are taken on trust, by students who do not have the time to check the evidence for themselves, on the authority of the distinguished people who proclaim them. The process has been well described by Charles Dickens in *Barnaby Rudge*. There was an oral tradition that Queen Elizabeth had used a mounting block in front of the Maypole Inn. This tradition was regarded as apocryphal in some quarters; but whenever the landlord appealed to the mounting block itself as evidence and triumphantly pointed out that there it stood in the same place to that very day, the doubters never failed to be put down by a large majority. For Mr. Willet the landlord was a very persuasive man. As he said himself,

> "If Natur has gifted a man with powers of argeyment, a man has a right to make the best of 'em, and has not a right to stand on false delicacy, and deny that he is so gifted; for that is a turning of his back on Natur, a flouting of her, a slighting of her precious caskets, and a proving of one's self to be a swine that isn't worth her scattering pearls before."[42]

Neill himself was not immune to the influence of persuasive people. After pointing out several weaknesses in the theory and methods of the form critics, he declared that, in spite of these, it was "impossible" that all the careful study they had directed to the gospels should prove to be without value.[43] I cannot follow his logic in saying this. Form criticism claims to be a scientific method of study. This claim, like all such claims, needs to be tested. If the tests show that the method is indeed scientific, then its results are likely to be of great value. But if the tests show that the method is not scientific, why should we expect careful study using unsound methods to be of any value whatsoever? Unless, of course, we mean that the work of the form critics was valuable in the way Dr. Watson was valuable to Sherlock Holmes:

> "I am afraid, my dear Watson, that most of your conclusions are erroneous. When I said that you stimulated me I meant, to be frank, that in noting your fallacies, I was occasionally guided towards the truth."[44]

For theories advocated by persuasive people (such as Dickens's Mr. Willet) to become axioms, what is needed is not fresh evidence but lapse of time. Herbert Butterfield recalled a remark made by Heisenberg that illuminates this process. In Heisenberg's opinion a scientist did not actually have to prove his theories; he merely had to wait for the coming of a new generation, which, starting from rather

---

[42]Charles Dickens, *Barnaby Rudge* (London: Chapman and Hall, n.d.) 1-8 (ch. 1).

[43]Neill, *Interpretation*, 243.

[44]Arthur Conan Doyle, "The Hound of the Baskervilles" in *Long Stories*, 243.

different presuppositions and viewing things from a different standpoint, would be more open to the acceptance of new ideas. Butterfield suggested that the same principle applied to the Arts subjects. The debate was not always thoroughly fought out, the argument not really clinched, because a geological subsidence had changed the whole situation—a new mentality, a new race of people had come on the stage.[45]

The only remedy against this tendency is to insist, as Morna Hooker insists, that the questions asked by one generation must be asked afresh by the next:

> The New Testament scholar must not simply set certain questions aside as "solved," but like a juggler endeavour to keep all his balls in the air—sometimes, indeed, adding new ones to the number in play, but never allowing any of them to drop.[46]

Take, for example, the theory that Mark's is the earliest of the four gospels. This is certainly the dominant hypothesis today—most scholars accept it and use it as a presupposition for further research. But this does not make it an "assured result." Insofar as it is possible to test the hypothesis, by comparing Mark's gospel with the other gospels, the facts can be shown to be consistent with the hypothesis—in Popper's words, they do not falsify it. But they can never verify it. Various scholars have shown that an alternative hypothesis—that Matthew's gospel was written before Mark's—is also consistent with the facts, if the facts are interpreted differently. Their contribution to the debate was welcomed by H. G. Wood. He believed that scholars were so accustomed to regarding the priority of Mark as an assured result that they had almost forgotten the evidence that established the conclusion:

> It is just as well that this confident assumption should be challenged if only to arouse us from what John Stuart Mill called "the deep slumber of a decided opinion."[47]

Let me illustrate the influence of unproved axioms in the making of scholarly decisions. In his book *A New Quest of the Historical Jesus* J. M. Robinson discussed the question, Did Mark have any knowledge of the chronology of the life of Jesus? This question has been answered in very different ways by two scholars. According to K. L. Schmidt, Mark arranged individual stories and sayings on a

---

[45]Herbert Butterfield, *The Discontinuities between the Generations in History* (Cambridge: Cambridge University Press, 1971) 5.

[46]Morna Dorothy Hooker, "In His Own Image?" in *What about the New Testament,* ed. Morna Dorothy Hooker and Colin J. A. Hickling (London: SCM Press, 1975) 28.

[47]Herbert George Wood, *Jesus in the Twentieth Century* (London: Lutterworth Press, 1960) 40.

topical basis, without interest in, or knowledge of, the actual sequence of events. According to C. H. Dodd, Mark used a chronological outline of the life of Jesus as a framework for his gospel. How do we decide between these two views?[48]

Robinson decided between them by using two different methods of assessment. In the case of K. L. Schmidt's book (and the earlier book by W. Wrede on the Messianic Secret) he wrote,

> The basic theses of these works have not been disproved, and therefore must continue to be presupposed in current scholarship conversant with them.[49]

In other words, they are axioms created by lapse of time—unproved hypotheses upgraded to presuppositions by the next generation.

In the case of C. H. Dodd's thesis, Robinson rejected it on the grounds that Dodd was not able to provide any "objective indication" of the existence of a pre-Markan chronological outline of the life of Christ. While Schmidt's thesis was accepted because it had not been *disproved,* Dodd's thesis was rejected because it had not been *proved.*[50]

Why did Robinson assess these two hypotheses in such different ways? His concluding sentence tells us the reason.

> Dodd's whole thesis with regard to a kerygmatic chronology fails for lack of the confirming evidence required to establish a position which would reverse the course of scholarship, and thus move against the stream of current views as to the probabilities in the case.[51]

It would seem from this that the question whether a hypothesis requires confirming evidence, or merely the absence of refuting evidence, can be decided by seeing whether it runs with or against the stream of current scholarly opinion.

The Need for Longsightedness

When serious thinking is to be done, human beings are naturally shortsighted. The up-to-date opinions are the ones we see in front of us, the ones that are discussed in current books and periodicals and on the media, the ones we need to know to pass our exams. It is natural to concentrate on current issues. But there are two disadvantages in doing so. One is that we fail to learn from the past; the

---

[48]James McConkey Robinson, *A New Quest of the Historical Jesus,* Studies in Biblical Theology 25 (London: SCM Press; Naperville IL: Alec R. Allenson, 1959) 48-58.

[49]Ibid., 36.

[50]Ibid., 58.

[51]Ibid.

other is that we fail to look to the future. These two forms of shortsightedness are logically connected, for one of the clearest lessons we learn form the past is that the "assured results" of one generation are out-of-date in the next.

"We should probably anticipate," counsels W. G. Doty, "that subsequent generations will regard our interpretations as being just as quaint as we now consider medieval exegesis to have been."[52] In theory this is not hard to accept. We read books written many centuries ago and smile at the quaintness of the ideas and the language; and we realize that our own generation would be unique were it not to appear equally quaint in years to come. In practice, however, it is difficult to see our own prospective quaintness as clearly as we can see the documented quaintness of medieval writers.

Consider, for example, the attitude to witchcraft a few centuries ago. From around 1450 to 1750, thousands of people were executed as witches all over Europe. *The Hammer of Witches* by Jakob Sprenger and Heinrich Kramer, first published in 1486, saw sixteen German, eleven French, two Italian, and six English editions in the following two centuries. The theology of witch-hunting was widely supported by both Catholics and Protestants; but we today regard it as alien to our whole way of thinking. We are amazed that people thought in that way only three centuries ago.[53]

I wonder which of our twentieth-century ideas will seem as quaint to future generations as the theology of witch-hunting seems to us. I wonder, for instance, what our descendants will think of the beachcombing theory of gospel origins, according to which the gospel writers, ignoring the evidence of the original eyewitnesses who were their contemporaries, gathered up instead floating fragments of tradition from the early church. This theory is so preposterous that future generations may well be amazed at the way intelligent people were able to believe it. But it is difficult for those living in the twentieth century, even for those who are critical of some details in the theory, to see it as future generations are likely to see it.

Robert Burns once prayed for the gift to see ourselves as others see us.[54] It would be an even greater gift to see ourselves as people in the twenty-first century will see us. C. S. Lewis believed that all writers, even the unorthodox, shared to some extent the blindness of their age, and that posterity would locate the char-

---

[52]William G. Doty, *Contemporary New Testament Interpretation* (Englewood Cliffs NJ: Prentice-Hall, 1972) 105.

[53]Rossell Hope Robbins, *The Encyclopedia of Witchcraft and Demonology* (London: Spring, 1959, ⁶1970; New York: Crown Publishers, 1959) as quoted in John N. M. Wijngaards, "The Awe-Inspiring Reality of Christ's Silence," *Indian Journal of Theology* 24 (1975): 132-42.

[54]Robert Burns, "To a Louse" (1786) st. 8.

acteristic blindness of the twentieth century in an area where we had never sus-
pected it. His proposed antidote was the reading of old books—if possible, old
ones and new ones in equal proportions, or at least one old book to every three
new ones. He realized that respect for the past frees us from the tyranny of the
present.[55]

Another scholar who realized this was Vincent Taylor. C. L. Mitton has noted
in Taylor's commentary on Mark, "that happy blend . . . of a quick appreciation
of new ideas with the discernment which can distinguish the permanent from the
ephemeral element in them." There was also "a clear-sighted determination to
refuse to reject the old and familiar merely because it is not new."[56]

Typical of Taylor's approach is his article, published in 1926, on Alfred Loisy,
a New Testament scholar whose views were then new and up-to-date. Taylor drew
a comparison between the New Testament commentaries of Loisy and the recent
commentary on the Apocalypse by R. H. Charles. In the commentary on the
Apocalypse he could discover not only what Charles himself thought, but what
Wellhausen, Spitta, Erbes, Bousset, Loisy, and others had taught, what Charles
accepted from these writers, what he rejected, and why. In Loisy's volumes he
found little or nothing of this kind.

> Loisy crowds his own stage; in the body of his works you hear few opinions ex-
> cept his own. . . . A critic who never loses the scent is not really following it.[57]

Charles and Loisy represent two approaches to scholarship. If we follow
Loisy's method, the scholar is a bloodhound, who never loses the scent until the
quarry is tracked down. If we follow Charles's method, the scholar is a mongrel,
whose eagerness to investigate smells old and new in a spirit of disinterested inquiry reflects the varied strains that have contributed to his or her own pedigree.

It was the mongrel approach to scholarship that Marc Bloch endorsed. He
looked forward to the day when the value of a science would be measured in proportion to its willingness to make refutation easy, and saw the "finicky little references" which abound in works of scholarship as working towards that day.[58]

The scientific approach is based on humility. It recognizes that our ignorance
always exceeds our knowledge, and that the latest opinion on any subject is just

---

[55]Clive Staples Lewis, "On the Reading of Old Books," in *First and Second Things*
(London: Collins, 1985) 27.

[56]C. Leslie Mitton, "Vincent Taylor: New Testament Scholar," introduction to *New
Testament Essays* by Vincent Taylor (London: Epworth Press, 1970) 21.

[57]Vincent Taylor, "The Alleged Neglect of M. Alfred Loisy," in ibid., 81.

[58]Marc Bloch, *The Historian's Craft* (Manchester: Manchester University Press, 1954)
88.

as limited, and just as likely to be wrong, as any that have preceded it. F. J. A. Hort saw clearly that the desire to be up-to-date was a denial of the very nature of scholarship:

> It has been well said that it belongs to a University to be a refuge for unpopular doctrines, the storehouse where truths long said to have been exploded are preserved from oblivion until their hour comes round again. This is to claim for a University the high privilege of escaping subjection to each surging wave of opinion as it hides the ocean before it follows its predecessor out of sight . . . and of maintaining . . . that cause which finds fewest spokesmen in the world without.[59]

---

[59]As quoted in Rupp, *Just Men*, 165.

The Argument
from Probable Certainty   2

"A guess is a particular and definite conclusion deduced from facts which properly yield only a general and indefinite one."   —Dr. Thorndyke[1]

The argument from probable certainty treats matters that are uncertain as if they were certain on the grounds of their probability. Those who employ this argument in New Testament studies realize that it is not possible to "prove" what exactly happened more than 1,900 years ago. But in their opinion some theories about the composition of the New Testament can be regarded as virtually certain, even though they cannot be logically proved. Those who express doubts about these theories are regarded as having closed minds, since anyone with an open mind will recognize a certainty when he or she sees it.

In the past, pressure to accept probable certainties has usually been exerted in support of traditional orthodoxy—the doctrines of the historic creeds and confessions of faith. In the twentieth century pressure is also sometimes exerted in support of modern critical orthodoxy—the "assured results of modern criticism." In both cases the reason behind the pressure is the genuine belief of the pressurizer that the dogmas concerned are sufficiently certain to warrant it.

I do not intend to discuss the "certainties" of traditional Christian orthodoxy. The doctrines of the historic creeds have been much debated in the twentieth century, and it is widely agreed that both those who acknowledge them and those who reject them do so by faith. What I wish to suggest is that some of the affirmations of modern critical orthodoxy are just as unprovable, and depend upon faith just as much, as the affirmations of the Athanasian Creed.

Let me illustrate this from Reginald Fuller's *Critical Introduction to the New Testament*. Fuller comments on the authorship of the Pastoral Epistles (1 and 2 Timothy and Titus) as follows:

---

[1]Richard Austin Freeman, *The Red Thumb Mark* (Bath: Lythway Press, n.d.) 112.

RSV and NEB contain thirteen letters ascribed to the apostle Paul. Of these, the Pastorals . . . are quite certainly later than Paul (though there are a few scholars who still argue for their Pauline authorship).[2]

This statement is amplified later in the book, where the author argues that the Pastoral Epistles

might have been included among the "disputed letters" of Paul . . . since there are some reputable scholars, notably J. Jeremias and J. N. D. Kelly who still maintain their Pauline authenticity. But the overwhelming majority of critical scholars, the English-speaking world included, regard them as deutero-Pauline.[3]

At first sight the words "quite certainly" seem out of place in discussing an issue of this sort. Scholars disagree as to whether or not Paul wrote the Pastoral Epistles. The disagreement is not about questions of fact. The facts—the contrast in style and subject matter between the Pastorals and Paul's letters to churches—are not in dispute. The area of disagreement lies in each scholar's assessment of whether one man would be capable of writing in such different ways in different circumstances. In other words, my belief or disbelief in Pauline authorship is a personal judgment, a leap of faith. How, then, can Fuller be "quite certain" when evaluating the personal judgments of other scholars?

I can think of four possible sources of this absolute certainty.

(1) *The argument from statistics.* Jeremias and Kelly are in a small minority, and therefore their opinion may be disregarded. On any given issue the "overwhelming majority of critical scholars" is bound to be right.

(2) *The argument from up-to-dateness.* The opinion of Jeremias and Kelly may be disregarded because it is old-fashioned. Fuller's repeated use of the word "still" implies this. In spite of what modern scholarship has shown, Jeremias and Kelly "still" maintain the old view. Their belief in Pauline authorship must be vestigial—a sign that they have not thrown off the conservatism of their Lutheran or Anglican backgrounds. It is like the vestigial tail human beings still maintain to prove they were originally monkeys.

(3) *The argument from reputation.* Jeremias and Kelly are "reputable scholars." But on this issue they have aligned themselves with the disreputable scholars who hold the traditional opinion. Therefore their judgment should not be taken seriously. This argument is a form of damnation by association.

---

[2]Reginald Horace Fuller, *A Critical Introduction to the New Testament* (London: Gerald Duckworth & Co. Ltd., 1966) 5.

[3]Ibid., 133.

(4) *The argument from conviction.* The author feels a deep inner conviction in his bones. His statement that the Pastorals are quite certainly later than Paul really means, "I feel quite certain in my own mind that Paul could not have written them."

Scholars who treat uncertain matters as if they were certain may be influenced by any or all of these arguments. But none of them is valid as a basis for certainty. They all seem to be deductions from generalizations. For example, the rule that the overwhelming majority of critical scholars is bound to be right is a generalization upgraded into a law. In this chapter I propose to raise some questions about the use of laws based on generalization, in historical study in general, and in the study of the New Testament in particular.

The Place of Law in Modern History

In E. H. Carr's opinion, the modern historian has abandoned the search for basic laws, and is content to inquire how things work.[4] This statement reflects the change in scientific attitude brought about in the twentieth century by Einstein and others. As Marc Bloch has declared, we are now more willing to admit that a scholarly discipline can be scientific without insisting on Euclidian demonstrations or immutable laws of repetition. We find it easier to regard certainty and universality as questions of degree.[5]

A pioneer of this attitude was the great historian Edward Gibbon. J. H. Plumb has described how Gibbon

> frequently spoke of the candour of history, because it could display, not truths about the universe, or immutable laws of social development, but merely the truth of ourselves as living human beings. History contained causes and events, not laws or systems.[6]

This does not mean that historians should not generalize. In E. H. Carr's judgment, history thrives on generalizations. What is wrong is to expand these generalizations into "some vast scheme of history into which specific events must be fitted."[7]

---

[4]Edward Hallett Carr, *What Is History?* (Harmondsworth: Penguin Books; New York: Viking Penguin Inc., 1964) 60.

[5]Marc Bloch, *The Historian's Craft* (Manchester: Manchester University Press, 1954) 17.

[6]John Harold Plumb, *The Death of the Past* (London: Macmillan, 1969; Boston: Houghton Mifflin, 1970) 130.

[7]Carr, *What Is History?*, 64.

There are at least two reasons why generalizations should not be upgraded into laws.

(1) *It is impossible to prove a general truth from particular instances.*

Generalizing from particular instances is an instinctive method of argument. We live in an ordered world in which, as the preacher said long ago, there is nothing new under the sun (Ecclesiastes 1:9). The experiences we have and the facts we learn are not isolated experiences and facts. They are particular examples of the way the world works as a whole. It is therefore tempting to assume that the facts we have found to be true in one case will be true in every case.

This was the method of argument used by the gang of boys called the Outlaws in Richmal Crompton's book *William the Gangster*. William's Aunt Jane, who was shortly to come on a visit, was recovering from a nervous breakdown, and the Outlaws were wondering how people who had suffered a nervous breakdown were likely to behave.

> "They carry on same as if they were mad," Ginger informed him. "They're jus' 'xactly like lunatics."
>
> "No, they don't," Douglas contradicted. "I know 'cause our cook once knew one an' I asked her what they were like an' she said that they laugh and cry all day long—first one then the other."
>
> "No, they don't do that," said Henry. "They throw things about. I know 'cause I met a boy that knew one. They don't laugh or cry or carry on mad or anything like that. They jus' throw things about."[8]

The Outlaws had grasped one of the basic principles of form criticism. Illnesses, like the sayings of Jesus, can be classified into various categories, each having its own set "form." One of these categories is the nervous breakdown. Therefore, all people having nervous breakdowns must behave in a predictable way. The experience of one person who has suffered a nervous breakdown can properly be used as a model to predict the behavior of any other sufferer. Anyone not following the correct "form" has not had a genuine nervous breakdown. The variety in the conclusions reached by the Outlaws is a confirmation of the soundness of their form-critical methodology.

The remark attributed by Shakespeare to Julius Caesar carries the method a step further:

> Let me have men about me that are fat, . . .
> Yond Cassius has a lean and hungry look,
> . . . such men are dangerous.[9]

---

[8]Richmal Crompton, *William the Gangster* (London: Collins, 1971) 91.

[9]William Shakespeare, *Julius Caesar* 1.2.191-94.

Caesar's judgment was presumably based on observation of many people over many years. He had found by experience that lean people were more dangerous than fat people. His argument might seem at first sight to be a logical advance on that of the Outlaws. He was generalizing from many instances; they were each generalizing from only one instance. But is it really an advance? To establish the truth that lean people are more dangerous than fat people, Caesar should have given some physiological evidence, showing for example the correlation between brain function and body fat. Without such evidence, no accumulation of particular instances could prove his point. As Dorothy Sayers observed, "the first man sinned, and laid the blame upon his wife; but it would be an error to conclude that all men, when they sin, blame their wives—though in fact they frequently do."[10]

(2) *Laws are more relevant to machines than to human beings.*

On the whole, machines are predictable. It is true that no two cars from the same assembly line will behave in precisely the same way. But in general, if you follow the instructions in the manual, your car will do what it is programmed to do. Human beings are not so predictable.

One of A. E. Housman's objections to the application of rigid rules in textual criticism was that scribes copying manuscripts were human beings. Textual criticism, he declared, is concerned with the frailties and aberrations of the human mind, and of its insubordinate servants, the human fingers. A textual critic is not like Newton investigating the motions of the planets; he is much more like a dog hunting for fleas. If a dog hunts fleas on mathematical principles, basing his researches on statistics of area and population, he will catch a flea only by accident. Fleas must be treated as individuals. In the same way, Housman asserted, every problem that presents itself to the textual critic should be regarded as possibly unique.[11]

Gerald Durrell, in his *My Family and Other Animals,* has described his childhood in Corfu. He seems to anticipate that his readers will find it difficult to believe what they read, that they will judge, by analogy with their own experience, that the events described could not have happened. He therefore explains that living in Corfu in those days was like living in a flamboyant and slapstick comic opera. The atmosphere of the place was summed up on a naval map they had, which showed the island and adjacent coastline in great detail. At the bottom of the map was a little inset which read,

---

[10]Dorothy Leigh Sayers, *Unpopular Opinions* (London: Victor Gollancz, 1946) 188.

[11]Alfred Edward Housman, *Selected Prose* (Cambridge: Cambridge University Press, 1961) 132, 133.

CAUTION: As the buoys marking the shoals are often out of position, mariners are cautioned to be on their guard when navigating these shores.[12]

The early Christians may not have been as flamboyant as Gerald Durrell's childhood friends. But they were human beings; and wherever human beings are concerned, scholarly map-readers should be on their guard.

The Place of Law in New Testament Scholarship

How far do New Testament scholars share the attitude to "laws" of twentieth-century historians? In the opinion of J. A. Baird, very little. Baird refers to the assumption made in modern works on mathematics and probability that all the scientist can talk about is the probability that some conclusion is accurate, and goes on:

To see how far New Testament exegesis is from this ideal, one has only to pick up almost any commentary and read at random: "without a doubt," "there can be no question," "it is obvious that," "it is absolutely certain." There is no field of human thought further from scientific discipline, at this moment, than that of biblical exegesis.[13]

Now Baird's statement is itself a generalization, and needs to be tested. New Testament scholars, like penguins, are not so much alike as may appear at first sight. Some are more cautious than others. What I propose is to give examples of laws (written or unwritten) to which appeal has been made by some New Testament scholars, and also to note some of the criticisms of these laws made by other scholars.

The Law of Fixed Forms. Agatha Christie's detective, Mr. Parker Pyne, was a great believer in human predictability. His method was one of prediction by classification. "I don't guess," he claimed, "I observe—and I classify."[14] On one occasion he was discussing with his client, Mrs. Packington, her husband's involvement with another woman:

"And doubtless he deplores the fact that women are so jealous, so unreasonably jealous when there is absolutely no cause for jealousy."
Again Mrs. Packington nodded, "That's it." She added sharply: "How do you know all this?"

---

[12]Gerald Durrell, *My Family and Other Animals* (Harmondsworth: Penguin Books, 1959) 11.

[13]Joseph Arthur Baird, *Audience Criticism and the Historical Jesus* (Philadelphia: Westminster Press, 1969) 30.

[14]Agatha Christie, *Parker Pyne Investigates* (London: Collins, 1962; [1]1934) 118.

"Statistics," Mr. Parker Pyne said simply.[15]

Mr. Parker Pyne's method of observing and classifying is also employed by the form critics. They believe the stories about Jesus and reports of his teaching were circulating for years in the early church before being written down, and in the process were considerably changed from their original version. They also believe they can reconstruct the way these changes took place, because there were fixed forms of storytelling in the ancient world and the early Christians must have employed these fixed forms. The most famous of the form critics, Rudolf Bultmann, wrote a *History of the Synoptic Tradition* (1921), based on what he called "the laws that govern literary transmission."[16]

Bultmann's starting point was "the observed fact that all literary presentations, particularly in primitive culture and in the ancient world, follow relatively fixed forms. This is true not only of written narratives, but also of oral tradition."[17] Therefore any variation from the fixed form of a story was in Bultmann's eyes a sign that the intruding element was "secondary"—added by the early church as the story was told and retold.

One of Bultmann's classifications of the gospel material was the controversial discourse. In such discourses, he believed, the dialogue always proceeded in crisp and trenchant form. The saying of Jesus contained the complete refutation of the opponent. Therefore, wherever in the Synoptic Gospels controversial sayings were followed by further elaboration, Bultmann regarded the elaborating words as "secondary."

For example, in Mark 2:19-20 Jesus replied to the question about his disciples fasting with the crisp and trenchant saying, "Can the bridegroom's friends fast when the bridegroom is with them?" According to Mark, he then continued with speculation about what the friends would do when the bridegroom goes away. In Bultmann's opinion these remarks, being elaborations, must have been added by the early church.[18]

The essence of this method of argument is to turn generalizations into laws. Bultmann's "laws that govern literary transmission" are generalizations based on analogy. Students of folklore in other cultures, or of the teaching methods of Jew-

---

[15]Ibid., 9.

[16]Rudolf Karl Bultmann, "The New Approach to the Synoptic Problem" in *Existence and Faith: Shorter Writings of Rudolf Bultmann,* trans. Schubert M. Ogden (London: Hodder & Stoughton, 1961) 39-66; (Cleveland and New York: World Publishing Co./Meridian Books, 1960) 35-54. (Note that the pagination in the USA edition differs from that of the British.) The phrase "the laws that govern . . . " is on 46 (British), or 41 (USA).

[17]Ibid., 45 (USA 40).

[18]Ibid., 50-51 (USA 45-46).

ish rabbis, have shown that stories and teaching in those cultures were commonly transmitted in certain forms. Bultmann assumed the stories in the gospels must have begun in these forms. Any gospel story that does not follow the norm must have been corrupted from its original purity of form by the early church.

The legalism of this approach is similar to the legalism of the Pharisees. Jesus had to remind the Pharisees that the sabbath was made for people, people were not made for the sabbath, and that he himself was master of the sabbath. Similarly, forms of speech are designed for people, people are not designed to be tied down by forms of speech, and Jesus was master of the language he used. The idea that Jesus would utter a crisp and trenchant saying and then keep his mouth shut for the rest of the evening belongs to the academic fantasy world. One wonders whether Bultmann had ever attended that modern equivalent of the controversial discourse situation, a press conference.

Form criticism has been practiced by two main groups of people—biblical scholars and gamblers at racecourses. The methods of the two groups are broadly similar. Gamblers predict the "form" of a horse by analyzing its form in previous races. If the analogy with previous races holds good, the favorite will win. In the same way New Testament scholars with a gambler's mentality have worked out by a study of form what Jesus and the early Christians are likely to have said and done. Those who have a system, like Bultmann, have talked not of probabilities but of certainties. In horse racing favorites do not always win, because analogies do not always hold good. The question raised by form criticism is, Were Jesus and the early Christians more predictable than racehorses?

The Law of Secondary Additions. The reasoning behind the law of secondary additions is simple. When people tell stories, they tend to add extra details. Therefore any details that appear in a story in Matthew or Luke, but do not appear in the same story in the (supposed) earlier Gospel of Mark, must be presumed to be early Christian additions. The common tendency to invent extra details when telling stories is turned into a law that all extra details must be inventions. An example of this law in operation is the following passage from Bultmann:

> In the later legends it is to be observed . . . that names are sought for many people whom the gospels mention without naming them. . . . Such legendary creations of the imagination are also to be observed in the gospels. Who were the two disciples mentioned in Mark 14:13 whom Jesus sent on before to prepare the Passover meal? In Luke 22:8 we have their names: Peter and John.[19]

Now on the assumption that Luke was using Mark as his main source, the question certainly arises: Where did Luke discover these names that are not in

---

[19]Ibid., 47 (USA 42).

Mark? But the answer is not so simple. He could have got the names from his own imagination, or from someone else's imagination, or from the evidence of an eyewitness. There is nothing in the story to show which of these explanations is correct. Bultmann assumed the names were a legendary creation of the imagination on the grounds, not of evidence, but of dogma: imaginative additions commonly occur; therefore any additions should be presumed to be imaginative in any given case.

On the whole, the form critics credited such secondary additions to early Christian preachers and storytellers. Their successors, the redaction critics, stress the creative role of the gospel writers. In either case, the temptation is to argue more from dogma than from evidence. If Matthew or Luke record a saying differently from Mark, how can anyone tell for what reason they do so?

Let us take as an example Norman Perrin's discussion of Mark 9:1 ("until they see the kingdom of God come with power") and the parallel verse in Matthew 16:28 ("until they see the Son of man coming in his kingdom"). Perrin states that Matthew understood the saying in Mark to refer to the end of the world, and reformulated it accordingly, so that "Matthew leaves his readers in no doubt as to what it is they are to expect."[20] This is certainly one possible explanation of the difference between the two versions. But other explanations are equally possible. Matthew may have heard Jesus speak these words himself, or have known someone who did so. Both Mark's version and Matthew's may be brief extracts from a much longer discourse of Jesus, in which he talked both of the kingdom of God coming and also of the Son of man coming. According to Perrin we have only one means of access to what Jesus said—the words of Mark 9:1. Any differences from Mark in Matthew's version are evidence for what Matthew thought, not for what Jesus said. But once we accept the possibility that Matthew may have had other sources besides Mark, the fact that Matthew is later (if it is a fact) becomes less important.

Why are Bultmann and Perrin so sure the supposed later versions of the passages they discuss are based on invention rather than on information? Perhaps it is because they subscribe to the dogma "the earlier, the purer." This dogma, in the opinion of Dorothy Sayers, fails to recognize that the gospel writers were "real" authors capable, like any modern biographer, of tapping new sources of knowledge:

> How much more readily we may accept discrepancies and additions when once
> we have rid ourselves of that notion "the earlier, the purer," which, however
> plausible in the case of folklore, is entirely irrelevant when it comes to "real"

---

[20]Norman Perrin, *Rediscovering the Teaching of Jesus* (London: SCM Press; New York: Harper & Row, 1967) 16, 17.

biography. Indeed, the first "Life" of any celebrity is nowadays accepted as an interim document.[21]

The Law of Doctrinal Development. Human beings and institutions never stop developing. For instance, Paul's attitude to the second coming of Christ changed over the years, and the influx of Gentiles into the church forced the Jerusalem church to rethink its position. The law of doctrinal development turns this general tendency into a law, and sees in the New Testament a steady and uniform development from the simple preaching of Jesus to the "early catholicism" of the end of the first century and beginning of the second. Believers in this law try to fix the date of each New Testament book by assigning the ideas it contains to the appropriate stage in this development.

This mechanization of early Christian thinking did not appeal to C. S. Lewis. His deepest skepticism was aroused by the statement that something in a gospel could not be historical because it showed a theology or an ecclesiology too developed for so early a date. Such a statement, he felt, implied a kind of inside knowledge of the life and thought of the early church, and of the forward and backward surge of its discussion, which he did not feel he could claim even for his own thought or for that of his friends, let alone for communities of people who lived 1,900 years ago.[22]

J. A. T. Robinson registered a similar protest in his book *Redating the New Testament*. It has often been argued that some books of the New Testament must be dated more than forty years after the resurrection of Jesus because it would take more than forty years for the ideas in those books to develop. Robinson disagreed. He detected a wild variation in scholarly estimates of the early Christian spiritual growth rate, and concluded, "it is impossible to say a priori how long is required for any development, or for the processes, communal and redactional, to which scholarly study has rightly drawn attention."[23]

The Law of Motivated Bias. According to this law, the accuracy of any writing is dependent on the motive of its author. Decisions about whether particular statements of the author are correct or incorrect can therefore properly be made, not only in the light of historical evidence, but also in the light of the critic's assessment of the author's motivation.

Now it is perfectly true, as a generalization, that the motives of authors influence their selection and arrangement of their material and, in some cases, the

---

[21]Sayers, *Unpopular Opinions,* 27.

[22]Clive Staples Lewis, *Christian Reflections* (London: Collins, 1981) 204-205.

[23]John Arthur Thomas Robinson, *Redating the New Testament* (London: SCM Press; Philadelphia: Westminster Press, 1976) 15, 344.

accuracy of their statements. But a generalization is not a law. Lord Peter Wimsey saw clearly the limitations of the argument from motive:

> "The police . . . *will* hive off after motive, which is a matter for psychologists. Juries are just the same. If they can see a motive, they tend to convict, however often the judge may tell them that there's no need to prove motive, and that motive by itself will never make a case. You've got to show how the thing was done, and then, if you like, bring in motive to back up your proof."[24]

In books about the New Testament, criticism based on the reconstruction of motives is called *tendency criticism*. The German word *Tendenz* means "bias," and tendency criticism, as described by W. G. Kümmel, works on the principle that "the meaning of a document can be properly determined only by taking its purpose into consideration."[25] The nineteenth-century pioneer of this approach was Ferdinand Christian Baur.

Baur applied tendency criticism first to the Acts of the Apostles. In his opinion the main aim of the author of Acts was to play down the differences between Peter and Paul, and between Jewish and Gentile Christianity. Two books in the New Testament refer to the relations between Peter and Paul—Acts and Galatians. There has been much debate about how these two accounts fit together; but in Baur's view it is a mistake to try to fit them together. Given the purpose of the author of Acts, we should not expect him to be accurate, but to say what he was motivated to say. Paul, on the other hand, was an eyewitness of the events he described, and his version should be preferred.[26]

Baur then turned his attention to the gospels. Here again, the first question to be asked was, What did each respective author wish and have in mind? Only with this question, Baur believed, could we reach "the firm ground of concrete historical truth." If there were accounts of the same event in two or more gospels, we should ask what were the motives of the respective authors, and assume that the least motivated was likely to be the most accurate.[27]

John's gospel in particular seemed to Baur to be highly motivated, and therefore much inferior to the other three gospels as a historical source. According to

---

[24]Dorothy Leigh Sayers, *Busman's Honeymoon* (London: Victor Gollancz, 1972) 262.

[25]Werner Georg Kümmel, *The New Testament: The History of the Investigation of Its Problems*, trans. S. McLean Gilmour and Howard C. Kee (London: SCM Press; Nashville/New York: Abingdon Press, 1972) 134.

[26]Ferdinand Christian Baur, *Paulus, der Apostel Jesu Christi* (Stuttgart, 1845). Baur's argument is summarized in Kümmel, *The New Testament*, 133-37.

[27]Ferdinand Christian Baur, *Kritische Untersuchungen über die kanonischen Evangelien* (Tübingen, 1847) as excerpted and translated in Kümmel, *The New Testament*, 137-38.

W. G. Kümmel, "this recognition belongs to the abiding results of New Testament research."[28] Certainly Baur has had many followers in making this claim, though many scholars take his argument a step further. They believe the Synoptic Gospels are just as much theological tracts as John's gospel—their authors were equally motivated, and therefore equally inaccurate.

In the twentieth century Baur's approach has been extended to apply not only to the gospel writers themselves, but also to the early Christian preachers and storytellers from whom the gospel writers are believed to have got much of their information. Bultmann, for example, believed that the "controversial sayings" in the gospels were the ammunition used by members of the early church in their arguments with their neighbors. These early defenders of the faith were motivated by a desire to win their argument, not by a desire to place the sayings of Jesus in their correct historical setting. Therefore, in Bultmann's opinion, it is incorrect to regard such controversial utterances as accounts of actual historical scenes in the life of Jesus.[29]

Following the same principle, Ernst Käsemann states that the early Christians told the stories of Jesus not from historical interest but from "kerygmatic" interest. (The word "kerygmatic" is derived from the Greek for preaching; it means that the early Christians preached for a verdict.) This motive helps explain the low historical value of the stories they told. In Käsemann's estimation all we know about the life of Jesus is that he was reputed to be a miracle worker, that he claimed to be an exorcist, and that he was crucified under Pontius Pilate. Only scattered fragments of the teaching recorded in the gospels went back with any degree of probability to Jesus himself. "The preaching about him has almost entirely supplanted his own preaching, as can be seen most clearly of all in the completely unhistorical Gospel of John."[30]

Now there is a grain of truth in this approach. If you know the political standpoint of a newspaper editor, this may help you understand not only the political comment of that newspaper, but also its selection and presentation of factual information. Similarly, in the case of ancient documents, one must always reckon with the possibility that the faith of the authors and their sources has influenced both their facts and their opinions. What is wrong is to turn this possibility into a law—to assume that the reliability of an author or storyteller is logically related to his or her motivation. Such an assumption, however attractive to the amateur psychologist, should not be entertained by the scientific historian. There are at least two reasons for this.

---

[28]Kümmel, *The New Testament*, 139.

[29]Bultmann, *Existence and Faith*, 51 (USA 45-46).

[30]Ernst Käsemann, *Essays on New Testament Themes*, Studies in Biblical Theology 41, trans. W. J. Montague (London: SCM Press, 1964) 60.

(1) *It is normally impossible for a critic to know an author's motives.*

Of course, when the author explicitly states his or her motive—as Luke (1:1-4) and John (20:31) do—the critic is on firm ground (unless one rigorously applies tendency criticism and concludes the author had an ulterior motive for stating his motive). However, most critical estimates of motive are based, not on the author's statement, but on the critic's imagination. All too often the imagination of critics is more limited than that of the authors they are criticizing.

Authors may have various motives, all working at the same time, some conscious, some unconscious. But tendency critics routinely credit an author with one dominant motive, and regard that as excluding all the others. Martin Hengel has rightly described the historical narratives of the New Testament as "kerygmatic historical reports," combining the zeal of the preacher with the biographical interest of the reporter.[31] But for Bultmann or Käsemann the choice must be exclusive: if they are "kerygmatic," they cannot be historical. Thus the scope of an ancient author is artificially limited by the narrow imagination of his modern critic.

C. S. Lewis was very skeptical of attempts to reconstruct the motives of New Testament authors. The reason for his skepticism was his own experience. Reviewers of his books had often speculated on his motives for writing this or that. In his experience these guesses were almost always wrong. Yet, compared to scholars reviewing the books of the New Testament, the reviewers of his books had many advantages. They spoke the same language as he did and shared the same culture; whereas New Testament scholars were writing about books written in a different language and belonging to a different culture. Faced with these disadvantages, Lewis believed, biblical critics would need almost superhuman powers of discernment to fare better than modern book reviewers in reconstructing the minds of the authors they discussed.[32]

Moreover, when estimating the bias of ancient authors, modern critics themselves are biased. E. H. Carr has suggested that, if we are to think of history as a moving procession, the historian himself is part of the procession. The point in the procession at which he finds himself determines his angle of vision over the past. Carr saw in George Grote's *History of Greece* (1846–1856) and Theodor Mommsen's *History of Rome* (1854–1856, 1886) a projection into the past of the problems and hopes of nineteenth-century Europe:

> Indeed, I should not think it an outrageous paradox if someone were to say that Grote's *History of Greece* has quite as much to tell us today about the thought of the English philosophical radicals in the 1840s as about Athenian

---

[31]Martin Hengel, *Acts and the History of Earliest Christianity,* trans. John Bowden (London: SCM Press, 1979; Philadelphia: Fortress Press, 1980) 15.

[32]Lewis, *Christian Reflections,* 199-202.

democracy in the fifth century B.C., or that anyone wishing to understand what 1848 did to the German liberals should take Mommsen's *History of Rome* as one of his textbooks.[33]

If Carr is right, modern imaginative reconstructions of the motives of early Christians may tell us as much or more about the attitudes of the twentieth century as they do about the attitudes of the first century.

(2) *Even if we could establish an author's motives, this would tell us nothing about his or her accuracy.*

Accurate reporting is more a matter of temperament than of motive. It is no doubt true that the primary motive of early Christian preachers and storytellers was not academic historical research. But this does not mean that they would divorce the sayings of Jesus from their historical setting. The effect of a saying, like the effect of a jewel, often depends on its setting; and even in those cases where the setting was not essential to the saying, accuracy in reporting depends, not on the motives, but on the habit of mind of the reporter.

Next time I hear a preacher use an illustration, I shall *not* say to him, "Mr. Preacher, your primary motive in preaching this sermon was not historical research; therefore your illustration must be inaccurate." I shall assume that, if he is a person who is careful by nature, his illustration will probably be accurate; and if he is a person who is careless by nature, his illustration may be inaccurate.

Furthermore, an author writing for a verdict will often be more likely to succeed by telling the truth. Luke dedicated his gospel to a man called Theophilus— perhaps a well-educated Gentile who had shown an interest in, or been instructed in, the Christian faith. In his preface Luke promised to present Theophilus with a well-researched and accurate account of the life of Jesus. Whatever Luke's inner motives may have been, he realized that an educated inquirer would expect accuracy, and therefore promised to provide it.

To say this is not, of course, to decide the question as to whether Luke lived up to his professed aims, whether at specific points—such as his reference to Quirinius in chapter 2—his statements agree or disagree with what is known of Roman history at that period. Such historical questions must be decided on their own merits. The basis for deciding them is the historical facts, not the supposed psychology of the author.

Motive hunting diverts attention from fact to fantasy. One of the pet peeves of C. S. Lewis was the modern tendency to assess statements of fact by reference to their author's psychology. He nicknamed this "Bulverism." The inventor of this way of thinking was Ezekiel Bulver, whose destiny was determined in his childhood. At the age of five, Bulver heard his father state that two sides of a tri-

---

[33]Carr, *What Is History?*, 35-37.

angle were together greater than the third, to which his mother replied, "Oh, you say that *because you are a man.*" At that moment there flashed across young Ezekiel's opening mind the great truth that refutation was not a necessary part of argument. You should assume your opponent is wrong, rather than trying to prove him wrong. In this way, Lewis declared, Bulver became one of the makers of the Twentieth Century.[34]

F. C. Baur was a typical Bulverist. He claimed that by examining the motives of the New Testament writers we could reach "the firm ground of concrete historical truth." The reality is the exact opposite. Motive hunting is like hang gliding: it lifts us from the firm ground into the pure air of academic speculation; where we land depends on how the wind is blowing.

Conclusion

The appeal to law in New Testament study implies that the New Testament came into being in ideal laboratory conditions, and that the early Christians conformed to a predictable pattern. "Early Christians" are regarded not as individuals but as specimens of a type, like the "moderately active man," described by Magnus Pyke, who expends 2,750 calories of energy every twenty-four hours. This "moderately active man," Pyke comments, is not you or me or anyone else, but an abstraction produced by the research scientist. If you dig deep enough into the tattered notebooks in which the actual figures were written down, you will find the names of the people involved, the trouble they gave, the doubts as to whether they did or did not skip out for a sly bottle of beer. The average man may have shown a consumption of 2,750 calories, but some individuals may have been getting along perfectly well on 1,850 calories and others eating their way through 3,650 calories.[35]

The problem with expert predictions is that people do not always do what the experts think they ought to do. Pyke illustrates this from the field of town planning. In the 1950s and 1960s many British towns were radically redeveloped. Whole areas of a town were pulled down and rebuilt in an economical, efficient, and scientific way. The unfortunate result, Pyke observes, was that when the people came back to reinhabit the places where they were born they did not recognize them and, worse still—in spite of the heating, ventilating, soundproofing, and upgrading, all done on a proper scientific basis—they did not much like what they found.[36]

---

[34]Clive Staples Lewis, "Bulverism, or the Foundation of Twentieth-Century Thought" in *First and Second Things* (London: Collins, 1985) 13-18.

[35]Magnus Pyke, *There and Back* (London: John Murray, 1978) 112.

[36]Ibid., 28.

There has been a parallel development in New Testament studies. The twentieth century has seen many attempts to reconstruct the New Testament according to a proper scientific plan. The trouble is that the New Testament grew organically, like the old town centers before they were redeveloped. If the early Christians were to come back today, they would not recognize the bulldozed, reconstructed New Testament some scholars have created.

The Argument from Primitive Culture

3

Critics are much madder than poets. . . . And even though St. John the Evangelist saw many strange monsters in his vision, he saw no creature so wild as one of his own commentators. —G. K. Chesterton[1]

There are two main ways of thinking about the past. To some, the past seems curiously modern. They would agree with the judgment of J. D. Crossan, after his visit to the paleolithic cave paintings of the Dordogne valley, that "old and dead are alien terms in the world of art."[2] To others, the main characteristic of people in past ages was their misfortune in not living in the twentieth century. Such was the attitude of the Oldest Member of the Golf Club described by P. G. Wodehouse:

> "I attribute the insane arrogance of the later Roman emperors almost entirely to the fact that, never having played golf, they never knew that strange, chastening humility which is engendered by a topped chip-shot. If Cleopatra had been outed in the first round of the Ladies' Singles, we should have heard a lot less of her proud imperiousness."[3]

The different ways in which scholars approach the New Testament reflect these two attitudes. In the view of some scholars those who lived in New Testament times were basically people like ourselves. In the view of other scholars those who lived in New Testament times were primitive, in the sense that they could not understand the world properly. The purpose of New Testament scholarship, on the

---

[1]Gilbert Keith Chesterton, *Orthodoxy* (London: Collins, 1961) 17.

[2]John Dominic Crossan, *In Parables* (San Francisco/New York: Harper & Row, 1973) 14.

[3]Pelham Grenville Wodehouse, *The Heart of a Goof* (London: Herbert Jenkins, 1926) 153.

latter view, is not only to interpret the New Testament, but also to update and modernize it.

A pioneer of this approach was the nineteenth-century scholar David Friedrich Strauss. The publication in 1835–1836 of Strauss's *The Life of Jesus Critically Examined* has been described by Stephen Neill as "a turning point in the history of the Christian faith."[4] W. G. Kümmel agrees: the writings of Strauss and of his older contemporary F. C. Baur were in his opinion the decisive works that first presented "a consistently historical view of the New Testament."[5] It is therefore important to ask, What were the presuppositions of a book that has altered the course of New Testament scholarship?

Strauss believed the gospel writers were incapable of writing history as we understand it, of distinguishing between fact and fantasy. The gospels are full of myths—pious legends and ideas about Jesus which are presented as historical facts because the gospel writers did not know any better. The early church was

> a Church of Orientals, for the most part uneducated people, which consequently was able to adopt and express these ideas only in concrete ways of fantasy, as pictures and as stories, not in the abstract form of rational understanding or concepts.[6]

Because of this we should not look to the gospels for historical accuracy, which their authors, as "uneducated Orientals," were incapable of providing. In Strauss's opinion the supernatural birth of Christ, his miracles, his resurrection, and ascension were "eternal truths" rather than historical facts.

Strauss's argument was developed in William Wrede's book *The Messianic Secret in the Gospels,* first published in 1901. Wrede protested against the view that Mark had more or less clearly before his eyes the actual circumstances of the life of Jesus. In Wrede's opinion the Gospel of Mark should be classified not as history but as dogma. Mark's was "a type of authorship which somewhat gauchely tries to fashion history out of ideas." Wrede does consider the possibility that Mark, when presenting as historical facts what were really the beliefs of the early church, might "in his own way . . . have thought historically in them." But, he goes on, "for a painfully naive author of antiquity this is, of course, extremely improba-

---

[4]Stephen Charles Neill, *The Interpretation of the New Testament 1861–1961* (London/New York/Toronto: Oxford University Press, 1964) 12.

[5]Werner Georg Kümmel, *The New Testament: The History of the Investigation of Its Problems,* trans. S. McLean Gilmour and Howard C. Kee (London: SCM Press; Nashville/New York: Abingdon, 1972) 120.

[6]Ibid., 122, translating and quoting David Friedrich Strauss, *Das Leben Jesu, kritisch bearbeitet (The Life of Jesus Critically Examined)* vol. 1, 1835; vol. 2, 1836; 1 and 2, [4]1840).

ble.'' Mark's disadvantage in not having been born in the nineteenth century prevented Wrede from taking him seriously as a source of historical truth.[7]

Now Strauss and Wrede lived in the heyday of Western imperialism. Many people in their day believed that nineteenth-century Europeans were superior to all lesser breeds, whether of the past or of the present. But although their attitude to the gospel writers could be called a nineteenth-century attitude, its influence is still very much alive. Wrede's influence in particular has been immense. Rudolf Bultmann stated in 1930 that Wrede's book was ''the most important work in the field of gospel research in the generation now past.''[8] Bultmann made Wrede's approach a presupposition of his own work and taught others to do likewise. James M. Robinson, surveying the opinions of some of Bultmann's leading pupils in 1959, pointed out that the foundation of post-Bultmannian New Testament research was not form criticism, which by then had ''passed out of vogue,'' but the arguments of scholars such as Wrede and Karl Ludwig Schmidt in the generation preceding form criticism.[9] Thus Wrede can be called the methodological grandfather of modern critical orthodoxy. His contemptuous dismissal of Mark as a painfully naive author of antiquity has passed through the generations into the mainstream of twentieth-century thought.

A British representative of this tradition is Dennis E. Nineham. Nineham argues that it is vitally important to recognize the cultural difference between the nineteenth and twentieth centuries, on the one hand, and all previous ages on the other. We should not regard human beings in all ages as just so many members of a single group, with relatively superficial differences of appearance and customs (the belief implied in the doctrine of the noble savage). ''Today we cannot help being aware that the savage—primitive man as he really was—differed so much from us in his understanding of himself, his gods, and his world that it is at least as misleading as it is illuminating simply to lump us both together under the category 'human beings'.''[10]

Nineham is not, of course, suggesting that the authors of the books of the Bible were primitive savages; but he does believe they were primitive in some respects.

---

[7]William Wrede, *The Messianic Secret in the Gospels,* trans. J. C. G. Greig (Cambridge: James Clarke; Greenwood SC: Attic Press, 1971) 129-35.

[8]Rudolf Karl Bultmann, *Die Erforschung der synoptischen Evangelien* (Giessen: Töpelmann, 1930) 10; ET: *Form Criticism,* trans. F. C. Grant (Chicago: Willett, Clark, 1934) 22; quoted in Ned Bernard Stonehouse, *Origins of the Synoptic Gospels* (Grand Rapids MI: Eerdmans, 1963; London: Tyndale House, 1964) 168.

[9]James McConkey Robinson, *A New Quest of the Historical Jesus,* Studies in Biblical Theology 25 (London: SCM Press; Naperville IL: Alec R. Allenson, 1959) 36-37.

[10]Dennis Eric Nineham, *The Use and Abuse of the Bible* (London: Macmillan; New York: Barnes and Noble Books, 1976) 95.

He describes the Bible as "the expression, or at any rate an outcrop, of the meaning-system of a relatively primitive cultural group."[11] We should therefore not expect from the biblical documents a degree of historical accuracy which, he declares, "it was not possible for documents of that culture to possess."[12]

Now it is certainly true that we in the twentieth century are in many respects more knowledgeable than people in the first century. We know more than they knew about the age and size of the universe, about the causes and cures of diseases, and so on. But this does not mean we are more intelligent than they were in using the knowledge we have, nor does it mean our presuppositions about life in general are necessarily more valid than theirs. If we are to call people of the first century "primitive," we need to define clearly what we mean by that word.

Let us look at some of the definitions of the word "primitive" in *Chambers English Dictionary*.[13]

(a) "belonging to the beginning, or to the first times." No doubt, in relation to the Christian church, the New Testament period can rightly be called primitive in this sense.

(b) "that from which other things are derived." The Greco-Roman world can be called primitive in this sense also. Not only are many of our moral values derived from that period, but the roots of modern scientific inquiry can be found in the ancient Greek culture from which modern Western culture is descended.

(c) "(of a culture or society) not advanced, lacking a written language and having only fairly simple technical skills." This does not seem to be a suitable description of Greco-Roman society during the New Testament period.

(d) "antiquated, old-fashioned, crude." The main question raised by the argument from primitive culture is whether the New Testament writers were primitive in this fourth sense. I wish to examine two areas in particular in which the New Testament writers, and people living in the first century as a whole, are often thought of as antiquated and crude: their attitude to the world around them, and their attitude to history.

The First-Century Attitude to the World

The New Testament writers believed (along with most of their contemporaries) in things that are commonly doubted today. They believed in angels and demons, and in a God who works miracles, who speaks to people through dreams

---

[11]Ibid., 28.

[12]Ibid., 236.

[13]*Chambers English Dictionary* (Cambridge and New York: W. & R. Chambers Ltd. and Cambridge University Press, 1988).

and visions, and who is actively involved in nature. There are millions of people in the twentieth century also who believe in these things, though in Western countries they may be in a minority. By what criteria do we decide whether or not these beliefs are correct?

One possible criterion is the psychological one: these things should not be believed because twentieth-century people are incapable of believing them. R. A. Sider quotes the statement of Van A. Harvey that "we in fact *do not* believe in a three-story universe or in the possession of the mind by either angelic or demonic beings. . . . We cannot see the world as the first Christians saw it. . . . These beliefs are no longer practically possible for us."[14]

Sider agrees there is a problem here, but disagrees with Harvey's solution. Sider accepts that "modern man—or at least *some* modern men!—find it practically, i.e., psychologically, impossible to believe in miracles," but he goes on to ask, "Are the psychological difficulties of modern men a criterion of truth?"[15] Analysis of the beliefs of "modern man" may be a necessary task for psychologists and sociologists; but such analysis cannot determine whether these beliefs are correct or incorrect.

Another possible criterion is the evolutionary one. Peter Berger has criticized Rudolf Bultmann for his statement that those who use electricity and listen to the radio can no longer believe in the miracle world of the New Testament. In such an attitude, Berger argues, there is a hidden double standard. The New Testament writers are seen as afflicted with the false consciousness of the past, but the contemporary analyst takes the consciousness of the present as an unmixed intellectual blessing. The electricity and radio users are placed intellectually above the apostle Paul.[16]

The antidote to this, in Berger's opinion, is to see both past and present in the light of sociology:

> Sociology frees us from the tyranny of the present. . . . The German historian Ranke said that "each age is immediate to God," intending thereby to reject the vulgar progressivism that sees one's own moment in history as history's pinnacle. The perspective of sociology increases our ability to investigate whatever truth each age may have discovered in its particular immediacy to God.[17]

---

[14]Van Austin Harvey, *The Historian and the Believer* (New York: Macmillan, 1966; London: SCM Press, 1967) 114.

[15]Ronald A. Sider, "The Historian, the Miraculous, and Post-Newtonian Man," *Scottish Journal of Theology* 25 (1972): 311.

[16]Peter L. Berger, *A Rumor of Angels* (New York: Doubleday, 1969) 51.

[17]Ibid., 56.

This is true not only when we compare the present with the past, but also when we compare different worldviews in the present. People who talk about twentieth-century culture usually mean the culture of modern Europeans or Americans, or at least of people susceptible to Western influence. But if we compare the modern Western worldview with the dominant worldview in other parts of the world, the contrasts can be just as striking as if we compare the present with the past.

In his book *The Primal Vision* J. V. Taylor has examined some features of African traditional religion. Many of these features can be paralleled on other continents, and in Taylor's judgment should be regarded as "the universal, basic elements of man's understanding of God and of the world." In describing these ways of thinking Taylor prefers the word "primal" to the word "primitive." The word "primitive," he writes, is "too suggestive of the popular but invalid transference of evolutionary theory to the realm of human ideas. . . . The profounder conversation that we have envisaged between the Christian and the pagan mind will be impossible so long as the former talks down as if to a child."[18]

We can see the attitude to which Taylor refers exemplified in G. K. Chesterton's character, Professor Chadd. The professor was talking to a retired judge, Basil Grant, about the Zulu people of T'Chaka. In a recent article Chadd had argued that they should be allowed to live in their traditional way, even though their stage in the evolutionary process was "definable in some degree as an inferior evolutionary stage." Basil Grant objected to this statement, and asked, "Why should a man be thought a sort of idiot because he feels the mystery and peril of existence itself? Suppose, my dear Chadd, suppose it is we who are the idiots because we are not afraid of devils in the dark?"[19]

Who are the real idiots? The New Testament writers did not know the discoveries of modern science, and their understanding of the world was thereby limited. But if we today assume that the only real world is the world of the scientist, our understanding is as limited as theirs. In Roland Frye's words, "the barbarian blindly asserts the primacy of his own temporal and cultural provincialism in judging and understanding and interpreting all that occurs, and the learned barbarian does precisely the same thing, but adds footnotes."[20]

Ernst Schumacher once paid a visit to Leningrad, during which he could not work out on the city map just where he was. He could see churches in front of him,

---

[18]John Vernon Taylor, *The Primal Vision* (London: SCM Press; Philadelphia: Fortress Press, 1963) 18.

[19]Gilbert Keith Chesterton, *The Club of Queer Trades* (Beaconsfield, England: Darwen Finlayson, 1960) 111.

[20]Roland Mushat Frye, "A Literary Perspective for the Criticism of the Gospels," in *Jesus and Man's Hope,* vol. 2 (Perspective 2), ed. Donald G. Miller and Dikran Y. Hadidian (Pittsburgh: Pittsburgh Theological Seminary, 1971) 198.

but these churches did not appear on the map he had been given. His Russian guide had to explain to him that they were willing to include on their maps church buildings converted into museums, but not "living churches." It then occurred to Schumacher that all through school and university he had been given maps of life and knowledge which failed to show many of the things he could see right in front of his eyes. These "maps" were deficient in two respects. They ignored the past because it was primitive; and they ignored everything in the present that did not fit in with the prevailing orthodoxy.[21]

As regards the past, Schumacher realized, the maps advised him that virtually all his ancestors, until a quite recent generation, had been pathetic illusionists who conducted their lives on the basis of irrational beliefs and absurd superstitions. As regards the present, the maps failed to show large "unorthodox" sections of both theory and practice in medicine, agriculture, psychology, and the social and political sciences, not to mention art and so-called occult and paranormal phenomena, the mere mention of which was considered to be a sign of mental deficiency.

The reason for this, Schumacher believed, was a "scientific imperialism" which made universal claims in the name of science for which there was no scientific basis.

> "The present danger," says Dr. Victor E. Frankl, a psychiatrist of unshakable sanity, "does not really lie in the loss of universality on the part of the scientist, but rather in his pretence and claim of totality. . . . What we have to deplore therefore is not so much the fact that *scientists are specialising,* but rather the fact that *specialists are generalising.*" After many centuries of theological imperialism, we have now had three centuries of an ever more aggressive "scientific imperialism," and the result is a degree of bewilderment and disorientation, particularly among the young, which can at any moment lead to the collapse of our civilisation.[22]

In my opinion the *belief* of people in the first century in angels, demons, and miracles has more claim to be called "scientific" than the *unbelief* of people in the twentieth century in angels, demons, and miracles. Their belief was based on evidence. For example, in the case of the man called Legion described in the gospels, the evidence consisted of the behavior of the man before he met Jesus and the change in his behavior after he met Jesus. The belief that Jesus had cast out demons was the most reasonable available explanation of this evidence.

---

[21]Ernst Friedrich Schumacher, *A Guide for the Perplexed* (London: Sphere Books, 1978) 9-14.

[22]Ibid., 13; the quotation is from Victor E. Frankl, "Reductionism and Nihilism," in *Beyond Reductionism,* ed. A. Koestler and J. R. Smythies (London, 1969).

The same could be said of ancient beliefs that have been demonstrated to be false by later discovery. Van A. Harvey cites the case of the ancient Greeks who rejected the view of Aristarchus that the earth moves round the sun. They rejected this theory on the grounds of the evidence then available. In the words of Toulmin and Goodfield, "insofar as they allowed their judgment to be influenced by the weight of the evidence, they can be said to have thought scientifically."[23] In the same way, since there was no evidence available in the first century to show that angels and demons did not exist, it would have been unscientific for a first-century thinker to deny their existence.

But how scientific is it to deny their existence in the twentieth century? Many today who deny the existence of angels, demons, and a miracle-working God base their unbelief, not on verifiable evidence of their nonexistence (which is unobtainable), but on the fact that people around them, or people who taught them at school or university, share that unbelief. One mark of a scientist is to be open-minded. Those who are willing to admit the possibility of angelic, demonic, or divine activity are more open-minded, and therefore more scientific, than those who are not.

It is a great temptation for scholars to believe that they can define what is impossible. They can fail to take note of Arthur C. Clarke's law:

> When a distinguished but elderly scientist states that something is possible, he is almost certainly right. When he states that something is impossible, he is very probably wrong.[24]

Take, for example, the attitude of some eighteenth-century scientists to reports that meteorites had fallen from heaven. On 13 September 1768 people in fields near Luce, France, saw a stone-mass drop from the sky after a violent thunderclap. The great physicist Lavoisier reported to the Academy of Science that the witnesses were mistaken or lying. Despite the evidence, the Academy would not accept the reality of meteorites until 1803.[25] Thomas Jefferson showed the same spirit when he said in 1807, "I could more easily believe that two Yankee professors would lie than that stones would fall from heaven."[26]

---

[23]Harvey, *Historian and Believer,* 117, quoting Stephen Edelston Toulmin and June Goodfield, *The Fabric of the Heavens* (London: Hutchinson, 1961; New York: Harper, 1962) 126.

[24]Arthur Charles Clarke, *Profiles of the Future* (New York: Harper & Row; London: Victor Gollancz, 1962) as quoted in Chris Morgan and David Langford, *Facts and Fallacies* (Exeter: Webb and Bower, 1981) 10.

[25]Morgan and Langford, *Facts and Fallacies,* 26, quoting the *Fortean Times.*

[26]Morgan and Langford, *Facts and Fallacies,* 26.

A scientist who refuses to take evidence seriously because the result is "impossible" thereby ceases to be a scientist. The same is true of a scientific historian, as Stephen Neill pointed out in his judgment of the nineteenth-century scholar Joseph-Ernest ("Ernst") Renan: "Renan started out to write the life of Jesus on the assumption that the supernatural does not occur; thereby he confessed in a sentence that he was not writing as a historian."[27]

Many scholars have followed Renan, and used the criterion of impossibility in deciding historical questions. Let me give an example from R. H. Fuller's *Critical Introduction to the New Testament*. Fuller is discussing those passages in the Acts of the Apostles that are written in the first-person plural (the so-called "we-sections"). He rejects the obvious explanation, that Luke has used "we" because he was an eyewitness of the events recorded in these sections, and gives as one of his reasons for rejection the following:

> Would a companion of Paul have inserted into the body of the "we" sections such obviously legendary material as the highly improbable account of the earthquake in the gaol at Philippi (Acts 16:26ff.)?[28]

On what grounds is this story labelled "legendary" and "highly improbable"? The improbability lies, I assume, not in the earthquake itself, but in the idea that God would use an earthquake to deliver Paul and Silas from prison. There could be two reasons for regarding this as improbable.

(1) *The form-critical reason.* Other stories of miraculous escapes were told in the ancient world, and this story represents an ancient tradition of escape-legend telling. If the other stories are legendary, this story must also be legendary. The truth of a story depends on the form in which it is told.

(2) *The primitive-cultural reason.* The idea that God would (or could) use an earthquake to deliver people from prison is too crude for the twentieth century. God, we now know, is a rational being, and if he guides us at all it must be in an intellectual way, not through natural phenomena. Because faith is cerebral, God's activity must also be cerebral.

Whether we think these arguments to be valid or not will depend on the point of view from which we start. One thing is clear: historical judgments of this kind reflect, not the expert knowledge of the scholars concerned, but their presuppositions.

---

[27]Neill, *Interpretation*, 281.

[28]Reginald Horace Fuller, *A Critical Introduction to the New Testament* (London: Gerald Duckworth and Co. Ltd., 1966) 130.

The First-Century Attitude to History

A popular theory today is the stratification theory of gospel origins. According to this theory the gospel writers, being too primitive to know the value of eye-witness evidence, turned instead to stories circulating in the early church. These stories contained layer upon layer of early Christian interpretation, laid down, like geological strata, over many years by successive storytellers. Dennis E. Nineham describes the process:

> When Matthew or Luke reproduce a passage from Mark they never do so in exactly the form in which he gives it. . . . Presumably Mark is related in the same sort of way to his sources, and they in turn to theirs, and so on back to the period of the Lord's own lifetime.[29]

The gospel critic, on this theory, is like a geologist. He has to distinguish the paleozoic stratum (the actual words and actions of Jesus) from the mesozoic strata (laid down by Jewish Christians in the Palestinian Christian era) and the cenozoic strata (laid down in the Greek-speaking Christian era). In the words of Amos N. Wilder,

> there are laws of form in social tradition as there are in geology. As Henry J. Cadbury has observed, to look beneath the surface in one of our gospels is like digging into an ancient mound: one finds successive strata, and in each of them distinctive and telltale objects and artifacts.[30]

Typical of this approach is Norman Perrin's remark that "an Aramaism can help us to reach an earlier stratum of the tradition"—in other words, if a gospel saying contains an Aramaic idiom, the stratum to which this saying belongs must have been laid down either in the mesozoic era, when the teaching of Jesus was being handed down by Aramaic-speaking Christians, or in the paleozoic era of Jesus himself.[31]

The use of geological metaphors to describe the origin of the gospels is, on the face of it, rather odd. Geological strata were laid down over millennia; the gospels were written in the same century as the events they record. One would never guess from Nineham's description of how Mark was related to his sources, and

---

[29]Dennis Eric Nineham, "Et hoc genus omne," in *Christian History and Interpretation*, ed. William R. Farmer, C. F. D. Moule, and R. R. Niebuhr (Cambridge: Cambridge University Press, 1966) 212.

[30]Amos Niven Wilder, *Early Christian Rhetoric: The Language of the Gospel* (London: SCM Press, 1964) 10; USA edition: *The Language of the Gospel: Early Christian Rhetoric* (New York: Harper & Row, 1964).

[31]Norman Perrin, *Rediscovering the Teaching of Jesus* (London: SCM Press, 1967) 37.

they in turn to theirs, and so on, that Mark wrote his gospel probably no more than forty years after the event, when hundreds of eyewitnesses of the ministry of Jesus were still alive. As I write these words in 1989, I am at a similar distance from the events of the Second World War. If I wished to write about a battle in that war, there are hundreds of people I could ask to give me an eyewitness account. Some would tell me in a British accent, some in an American accent, some in a German accent, some in other accents. The "form" of their accounts would differ, but they would all be eyewitnesses. Of course, I could ignore this evidence, and rely exclusively on barrack-room traditions. If I did this, it would not prove that "there are laws of form in social tradition," but that I was not fit to be a historian.

The modern theory is that Mark, when describing incidents that took place some forty years earlier, gained his information not from the original eyewitnesses such as Peter, who were alive and known to him, but from church traditions laid down in successive strata over the years. This theory is an insult to Mark's intelligence. It assumes that Mark, being a primitive person, could not be expected to know any better.

The primitiveness of the gospel writers is often regarded as typical of the age they lived in. Historical writing in the Greco-Roman world as a whole can be shown to be primitive by the following syllogism:

(1) Had the Greeks and Romans been our intellectual equals, they would have written the same kind of history as we do.

(2) Ancient history books were in fact written very differently from modern academic history books.

(3) Therefore, they were intellectually inferior to us.

The minor premise of this syllogism is broadly correct. Even though, as E. H. Carr has pointed out, there are very different approaches to the writing of history within the twentieth century itself, modern academic history does differ considerably from the history written in the ancient world.[32] The problem with the syllogism lies in its major premise, which fails to take account of other factors besides intellectual inequality that can help explain this contrast.

To highlight the differences between ancient and modern historians, let me quote the words of three twentieth-century scholars.

First, according to J. H. Plumb, "professional history of the twentieth century is as remote from the history produced by our ancestors as modern physics is from Archimedes." Of the great ancient historians Thucydides came nearest to seeing history in a twentieth-century way, but

---

[32]Cf. Edward Hallett Carr, *What Is History?* (Harmondsworth: Penguin Books; New York: Viking Penguin Inc., 1964) 40-44.

Thucydides was pursuing truths, not historical truth, but truths about men's behaviour in war and politics—the nature of man, the operation of chance, courage and weakness, good and evil—and therefore he permitted himself imaginative methods, such as his opposed dialogues, which are as alien to history as we know it as alchemy is to the scientist.[33]

Second, in the judgment of Erich Auerbach, "historiography in depth—that is, methodical research into the historical growth of social as well as intellectual movements—is a thing unknown to antiquity." Auerbach quotes the comment of Rostovtzeff in his *Social and Economic History of the Roman Empire* that "the historians were not interested in the economic life of the Empire."[34]

Third, Martin Hengel points out that writers of biography in the ancient world were not interested in two of the essential elements in modern biography: psychology and chronology. The aim of the ancient biographer was not to depict the psychological development of the hero against a clearly defined chronological background, but to work out the already established character of the hero and his predetermined fate. Chronological sequence played a secondary role. Authors were quite content to string together a series of typical anecdotes with virtually no connection between them.[35]

Such statements raise the question, Is the difference in style and method between ancient and modern historians a symptom of the primitive nature of Greco-Roman culture, or it is due to other factors? Let me suggest two ways in which the working situation of ancient and modern historians may be seen to differ, which may provide at least a partial explanation for these differences.

(1) *The availability of source material.* The modern historian has access to vast sources of information—books, microfilm, tape recordings, the documented research of other historians, a plethora of official records on almost all subjects. In the ancient world, however, as Martin Hengel says, "the abundance of information from all sides, which we take for granted, was simply not there. Reports were still in short supply."[36] Ancient historians did make good use of official records when they were available; but usually they had to rely on oral reports.

---

[33]John Harold Plumb, *The Death of the Past* (London: Macmillan, 1969; Boston: Houghton Mifflin, 1970) 108 and 20.

[34]Erich Auerbach, *Mimesis: The Representation of Reality in Western Literature,* trans. Willard R. Trask (Princeton: Princeton University Press, 1963) 38, quoting Mikhail Ivanovich Rostovtzeff, *The Social and Economic History of the Roman Empire* (Oxford: Oxford University Press/Clarendon Press, 1926) 88.

[35]Martin Hengel, *Acts and the History of Earliest Christianity,* trans. John Bowden (London: SCM Press, 1979; Philadelphia: Fortress Press, 1980) 15.

[36]Ibid., 13.

This was particularly true of public speeches. G. K. Clark observes that in the past it was not possible to obtain a word-for-word record of any speech. Sir Isaac Pitman, after reviewing all the shorthand systems of the early seventeenth century, came to the conclusion that it would not be possible for anyone using them to take down more than fifty to seventy words a minute, whereas an ordinary public speaker utters about 120 words to the minute, and a rapid speaker as many as 180 to 200 words.[37]

According to the *Guinness Book of Records* the greatest speaking speed recorded in public life was a 327-words-a-minute burst in a speech made in December 1961 by John Fitzgerald Kennedy.[38] A modern historian can quote accurately what Kennedy said on that occasion. An ancient historian was faced with the choice of either not reporting a speech, or basing his report on the evidence of a listener who remembered the gist of the speech, but not the actual words.

However, within the limitations of the source material available, ancient historians were well aware of the importance of reliable evidence. In the preface to his gospel Luke states that the accounts of the life of Jesus written up to that time were based on the evidence of eyewitnesses (this being, he implies, an accepted principle in his day). It was certainly an accepted principle in ancient history writing as a whole. In his book *The Nature of History in Ancient Greece and Rome* C. W. Fornara points out that the word "history" comes from the Greek ἱστο- ρία (Latin *historia*) which means "inquiry," "research," or "investigation," and that the definition typifies the method of the Greek historians. The method, as Fornara describes it, consisted basically of the interrogation of witnesses and other informed parties and of the redaction of the answers into a continuous narrative. Herodotus, by describing his work as "an exposition of his research," established the method as a principle of historical writing. Thucydides presupposed it as self-evident, and later writers "continued the practice as a matter of course."[39]

Many ancient historians wrote about events that took place within living memory, and their credibility depended on their accuracy. Polybius, for example, related how Lucius Aemilius Paullus had the disposal of vast treasures during his official career, but was so honest that he ended his life a relatively poor man. Polybius felt this might seem incredible to some readers, and explained that the Romans who would read his work would be aware of the facts, and would not be prepared to pardon an author who uttered false statements. His readers should bear

---

[37]George Sidney Roberts Kitson Clark, *The Critical Historian* (London: Heinemann; New York: Basic Books, 1967) 88.

[38]Norris McWhirter, ed., *The Guinness Book of Records,* 1980 edition (Enfield: Guinness Superlatives Ltd., 1980) 21.

[39]Charles William Fornara, *The Nature of History in Ancient Greece and Rome* (Berkeley: University of California Press, 1983) 47.

in mind, whenever he made a surprising statement about the Romans, that "nobody would willingly expose himself to their inevitable disbelief or contempt."[40]

In describing the Roman conquests in the Mediterranean, Polybius prided himself on his impartiality. He commented on two earlier historians—Philinus who was pro-Carthaginian and Fabius who was pro-Roman—that in other spheres of life such partiality could be commended. A good man should love his friends and his country and share their hatreds and their loyalties. But "once a man takes up the role of a historian he must discard all considerations of this kind." He should be willing to speak well of his enemies, and to criticize his friends.[41]

In Fornara's judgment, this impartial approach was not peculiar to Polybius:

> Of the various principles laid down by the ancients, none is more fundamental than the honest and impartial presentation of the facts, and it is entirely consistent with their clarity of vision and intellectual emancipation that the Greeks gave it to the world.[42]

(2) *The expectations of the audience.* If Agatha Christie were asked to comment on the manuscript of a budding writer of detective stories, the only piece of advice she would give would be to study the market.[43] The same advice would no doubt apply in the ancient world too; but the market situation would be very different.

Modern historians are able to write for an academic market, and their writings need not be of any interest to the general public. A doctoral thesis or an article in a learned journal will be read by a small number of specially trained people. The thesis will not be judged by its potential in paperback; nor will the low readership of the article affect the university salary of its author. This gives modern historians great freedom. They can support their statements with detailed footnotes, give all the evidence and assess all the previous interpretations, without worrying whether this will interest the general public or not.

In the ancient world, history writing was of two kinds. On the one hand there were the official records kept in the cities, such as the *annales maximi* kept in Rome by the pontiff. On the other hand there were private historians who wrote as individuals. According to A. Momigliano, in his essay "The Historians of the Classical World and Their Audiences," the distinction between these two types of history was especially marked in Greece. Whereas in Rome accepted members of

---

[40]Polybius (ca. 200–118 B.C.E.), *The Rise of the Roman Empire,* trans. Ian Scott-Kilvert (New York: Viking Penguin Inc.; London: Penguin Books, 1979) 527 (= 31.22).

[41]Ibid., 55 (= 1.14).

[42]Fornara, *Nature of History,* 99.

[43]Agatha Christie, *An Autobiography* (London: Collins, 1977) 334.

the ruling class were frequently its historians, in Greece the historians were often rejected politicians and exiles.[44]

Momigliano points out that ancient historians, unlike poets and orators, did not have a clearly defined audience. They arrived late on the market (in the fifth century B.C.E.) and were never certain of finding a buyer for their products. Not having a recognized place in society, they had continuously to repeat the claim that their histories were either instructive or pleasurable, because "the word 'history' did not by itself suggest either instruction or pleasure."[45]

What was the nature of the pleasure they offered? (Both Thucydides and Tacitus refused to give the pleasure that comes from fabulous stories.[46]) Ancient historians aimed to please their audiences in two ways.

(1) Their writing had to sound good, and to be suitable for reading aloud. According to Momigliano, "what little we know suggests that throughout classical antiquity it was customary to announce or to celebrate the publication of a work of history with a public reading." Momigliano cites several ancient historians who followed this practice, such as the second-century B.C.E. writer Aristotheus, who read aloud his pro-Roman work in Delphi for several consecutive days. Reading aloud was also a means of honoring a historian. For example, while the emperor Claudius was alive, his books in Greek on Etruscan and Carthaginian history were read at stated dates in the two museums of Alexandria.[47]

(2) Their writing had to appeal, in Polybius's words, to "those who take pleasure in the acquisition of knowledge."[48] He did not mean by this a pleasure in facts for their own sake. In Fornara's opinion the concept of history in the objective sense, as the aggregate of past events, was unknown to antiquity.[49] Ancient historians followed the lead of Herodotus, who conformed to the pattern of epic poetry in singing the κλέα ἀνδρῶν (*klea andrōn*)—the famous deeds of men: "This is the exhibition of the research of Herodotus of Halicarnassus, so that great and amazing deeds, some of them achieved by the Hellenes, others by the barbarians, might not lose their fame."[50]

---

[44]Arnaldo Momigliano, "The Historians of the Classical World and Their Audiences: Some Suggestions," ch. 25 of *Sesto Contributo alla Storia degli Studi Classici e del Mondo Antico, ,* Tomo Primo (Rome: Edizioni di Storia e Letteratura, 1980) 371.

[45]Ibid., 362.

[46]Fornara, *Nature of History,* 120.

[47]Momigliano, "Historians," 364.

[48]Fornara, *Nature of History,* 122. This is Fornara's translation of the Greek *philomathountes.*

[49]Ibid., 91.

[50]Ibid., 96.

This principle of selection was copied by later historians. Polybius, for example, explains his omission of Egyptian affairs in one section of his history on the grounds that Ptolemy had done nothing of moment: "This man, except for the cruelty and license of his court, performed neither a land battle nor a sea battle nor a siege of a city nor any other thing worthy of remembrance."[51]

One reason for this limitation of subject matter to great deeds was the interest of the audience. In a revealing passage Polybius states that he expects most of his readers to be Romans "since the greatest number and the most brilliant of the achievements which it describes belong to them."[52] As Martin Hengel says, ancient historians "simply presented what interested them and their readers, because they depended on the good will of their readers and wanted to instruct them, admonish them, and—also—entertain them."[53]

The closest modern parallel to the history books of the ancient world is not the books produced by academic historians for an academic readership, but the history presented to the general public by the mass media. Much of what David Edgar said in defence of drama-documentaries (so-called "docudramas") would apply equally to a historian such as Thucydides, and to his use of speeches and dialogues.[54]

Edgar took issue with those critics who saw a conflict between the drama-documentary and the high standards of objectivity one would expect from a professional historian. Following E. H. Carr, he was very dubious about the nineteenth-century notion of pure historical objectivity. But he did believe in the ability of dramatic fiction to illuminate certain areas of public life. In his opinion, no political analysis of the balance of forces in Czechoslovakia in the summer of 1968 could have re-created the atmosphere within the Czech politburo in the way that David Boulton was able to do in his drama-documentary *Invasion*.

The drama-documentary *Invasion* was no doubt inaccurate in the sense that the dialogue did not proceed word for word as it did in real life in 1968. Moreover, it was based mainly on the recollections of one person—Zdenek Mlynar, who was secretary of the Czech Communist Party Central Committee at the time. But it was as historically accurate as the dramatic form would allow, being based on careful research and on such eyewitness evidence as was available. And it conveyed the "feel" of the original events in a way that academic history could not. In these

---

[51]Ibid., 98, quoting Polybius, *Roman Empire* 14.12.

[52]Polybius, *Roman Empire*, 527 (= 31.22). This is referred to in Fornara, *Nature of History*, 92 n. 1, but the wording in the text is from Ian Scott-Kilvert's translation.

[53]Hengel, *Acts*, 18.

[54]David Edgar, "In Defence of Drama-Documentaries," *The Listener*, 1 January 1981, 10-11.

respects it followed the historical method described by Thucydides at the beginning of his *History of the Peloponnesian War*:

> With reference to the speeches in this history, some were delivered before the war began, others while it was going on; some I heard myself, others I got from various quarters; it was in all cases difficult to carry them word for word in one's memory, so my habit has been to make the speakers say what was in my opinion demanded of them by the various occasions, of course adhering as closely as possible to the general sense of what they really said.[55]

We remarked earlier that the early church historian Luke shared with Thucydides the ambition to be as accurate as possible. Luke also shared with Thucydides the desire to select and present his material in a way that would hold the attention of his readers. He did not have the freedom of the modern historian to discuss sources, or to justify his statements by scholarly footnotes. As a result, it is impossible for us to know where he got much of his information.

What, then, are we to make of dogmatic statements such as the following by John Knox?

> The gospels, in both intention and fact, are not the product of careful, critical research into the original facts, but are records of the Church's teaching: they bring us Jesus *as the early community thought of him.*[56]

It is impossible to prove or disprove a statement of this kind. Did Luke base his account of the birth of Jesus on personal conversation with Mary, or on an interview with one of the shepherds, or on uncritical acceptance of birth-stories that were circulating in the early church? Luke does not tell us his sources, and we can only guess them. Knox's claim to know how the gospel writers set about their work is not the product of careful, critical research into the original facts (since those facts are not known to us, and can only be conjectured); it is a record of the teaching of one school of modern criticism. It brings us Matthew, Mark, Luke, and John *as the form-critical community thought of them.*

Conclusion

In C. S. Lewis's book *The Screwtape Letters* the senior devil Screwtape recommends to his junior tempters various ideas for putting into the minds of human

---

[55]Thucydides, *The History of the Peloponnesian War,* trans. Richard Crawley (London: J. M. Dent, 1903) 11 (= 1.22.1). (Thucydides d. ca. 401 B.C.E.; he wrote his *History of the Peloponnesian War* sometime after 411 B.C.E.)

[56]John Knox, *The Church and the Reality of Christ* (New York and Evanston: Harper & Row, 1962; London: Collins, 1963) 15.

beings. One of these ideas is "The Historical Point of View." It consists of looking at ancient authors and asking who influenced them, and how they influenced others, and what scholars have said about them, but never regarding them as possible sources of truth, who could influence our thought or behavior today. The Historical Point of View, Screwtape argues, cuts every generation off from all others, and prevents that free commerce between the ages which can enable great scholars to be nourished by the past.[57]

The argument from primitive culture is of great help in promoting the Historical Point of View. It regards the New Testament writers as strangers, belonging to an alien culture which we have now outgrown. It is not appropriate for us to sit at their feet and learn from them, but rather to examine them from a distance, as a scientist peers through a microscope at a microbe. The books of the New Testament thus become, not sources of knowledge, but sources of problems; not quarries of truth, but seedbeds of debate.

We need to realize that the apostles were people who thought and reasoned much as we do today. Moreover, they were privileged to witness some of the most exciting events the world has ever known—the life, death, and resurrection of Jesus and the explosion into life of the early church. If we can be delivered from our feeling of cultural superiority and our fond belief that, compared to us, the early Christians were primitive, we can become free to sit at their feet, and to learn from them things that we in the twentieth century desperately need.

---

[57]Clive Staples Lewis, *The Screwtape Letters* (London: Geoffrey Bles, 1942; London: Collins/Fontana Books, 1955) 139-40.

The Argument
from Silence

4

"The dog did nothing in the night-time."
"That was the curious incident," remarked Sherlock Holmes.[1]

The argument from silence is often used in New Testament criticism. It works very simply. You look at a New Testament book and think of all the things that, in your opinion, the author of that book should have included; you note which of these things he in fact omitted; and you deduce from these omissions the author's doctrinal bias, or his mental condition, or the fact that the book was not written by that author at all.

This method of argument is attractive, because its conditions are laid down by the critic, not by the author. Most literary criticism is concerned with what authors write. The argument from silence, by contrast, is concerned not so much with what authors write as with what critics think they ought to write. It is therefore especially attractive to creative critics, who find the task of imagining what should be in a book more congenial than the task of understanding what is actually there.

The main weakness of the argument from silence is that it takes little account of the way books are actually written, and of the manifold pressures that force authors to leave out things they would like to include. Richmal Crompton provides a good illustration of this in one of her books about the boy William. William's friends, the Outlaws, are discussing Guy Fawkes, whose plot to destroy the Houses of Parliament is affectionately remembered by the British every November:

> "He must've done something else besides try to blow up the Gov'n-ment," said Ginger.

---

[1]Arthur Conan Doyle, "Silver Blaze," in *The Memoirs of Sherlock Holmes* (London: Penguin Books; New York: Viking Penguin Inc., 1950) 28.

"He didn't," said Henry. "That's all he ever did an' he got executed for it."[2]

Henry assumed all the events that happened in history had been recorded in the school textbooks. Only one action of Guy Fawkes was recorded; therefore, that was all he ever did. It takes time and maturity to realize that school textbooks, like every other kind of literature, are forced to omit far more than they include.

In this chapter I shall first discuss the "law of nonmention," which underlies the argument from silence. I shall then discuss the art of omission in literary composition in general and in the New Testament in particular.

The Law of Nonmention

The "law of nonmention" runs as follows: "If authors fail to mention things we should have expected them to mention, that silence must be significant. It may reflect their ignorance, or their unbelief, or their determination to suppress the truth." Let us look at a few examples of scholarly arguments that presuppose this law.

(1) *The authorship of 1 Peter.* According to the "law of nonmention," no book of the New Testament was written by the author whose name it bears unless it mentions all the ideas we should expect that author to mention. F. W. Beare's commentary on 1 Peter relies more than most on this method of argument.[3]

Beare observes that the Spirit of God is mentioned only four times in 1 Peter, and that none of these passages refers to the Spirit as dwelling within the believer. He regards this as a sign that 1 Peter is the product of a later generation, in which the sense of the active presence of the Spirit had fallen into eclipse.[4] Similarly, there is no discussion in 1 Peter of the question of justification by faith or by law, which Paul dealt with in some of his epistles. This proves, to Beare's satisfaction, that "if this man was a Jew, he had emancipated himself from his own religious inheritance to a degree that was never possible for Paul."[5] Strangely, Beare does not refer to the fact that there is also no mention of fishing in 1 Peter, which is difficult to account for if the author's background for most of his life was the fishing industry.

---

[2]Richmal Crompton, *William Carries On* (London: Collins, 1972) 94.

[3]Francis Wright Beare, *The First Epistle of Peter*, 2nd ed. (Oxford: Basil Blackwell, 1961) 35-36.

[4]Ibid., 35-36. On this J. A. T. Robinson commented that "seldom can the argument from silence have been made to cover so much," in *Redating the New Testament* (London: SCM Press, 1976) 162.

[5]Beare, *First Peter*, 27.

It is difficult to take such arguments seriously. First Peter is of similar length to a modern sermon. We can no more expect its author to refer to every major doctrine in the course of the letter than we could expect modern preachers to refer to every clause in the Nicene Creed in every sermon they preach.

One of Beare's arguments is especially interesting, in that he was forced to withdraw in his second edition an argument from silence used in the first edition. Many scholars think 1 Peter was written in Rome, since "Babylon" seems to be a codename for Rome in 1 Peter 5:13. In the first edition Beare rejected this view on the grounds that he could find no reference to the letter in the Latin churches until the time of Cyprian, and that it was not mentioned in the late-second-century Roman list of canonical books called the Muratorian Canon. However, by the time of the second edition he had become convinced of the links between 1 Peter and Hippolytus pointed out by F. L. Cross and of the links between 1 Peter and 1 Clement pointed out by Eduard Lohse. Beare's treatment of this question shows up the essential weakness of any argument from silence. It only takes one new discovery to demonstrate that the silence before the discovery was purely accidental, and that the argument built upon that silence was built upon sand.[6]

(2) *The person of Christ.* In his book *The Use and Abuse of the Bible* Dennis E. Nineham describes three ways of thinking about Jesus, all of which are to be found in the pages of the New Testament:

(a) Jesus was preexistent—He was already God's Son before being born on this earth.
(b) Jesus was the Son of God in the sense that God's Spirit was jointly responsible with a human mother for his birth.
(c) Jesus was a man, born into King David's family, who went about doing good and was able to perform miracles because God was with him.[7]

Theologians in the past have harmonized these three statements. According to the historic creeds, Jesus was both eternally divine and genuinely human. But in Nineham's opinion these three ways of thinking represent variant views about Jesus, held by different circles in the early church. Matthew and Luke included these variant views within their writings because of the disregard for consistency that is characteristic of primitive culture. They cannot be harmonized into a single coherent picture which could be called "the primitive Christian faith." "Christ's preexistence," Nineham declares, "is not an 'aspect' of someone who according

---

[6]Ibid., 31, 202.

[7]Dennis Eric Nineham, *The Use and Abuse of the Bible* (London: Macmillan; New York: Barnes and Noble Books, 1976) 151-63.

to Matthew and Luke, or at any rate most of their sources, had no existence at all before his birth from Mary!"[8]

Attempts such as this to drive a wedge between different New Testament "theologies" often rely on the argument from silence. Nineham states that Jesus, according to Matthew and Luke, did not exist before his birth from Mary. The only evidence for this statement is that Matthew and Luke do not *mention* his previous existence. They do not mention it; therefore they do not believe in it. Similarly, in Peter's speech in the home of Cornelius in Acts 10, Jesus is described as a man anointed by God, who could heal the sick because God was with him. In reporting this speech Luke fails to mention either the preexistence of Jesus or the involvement of the Holy Spirit in his birth. He does not mention these things; therefore, the argument runs, either he or his source or both do not believe in them.

By following this method it is possible to prove that almost any two statements are inconsistent with each other. For unless they repeat the same ideas in identical words, there are bound to be words and ideas contained in the one that are omitted in the other.

(3) *The Call of the Disciples.* The argument from silence was one of the tools used by the form critic Rudolf Bultmann to decide which material in the gospels went back to Jesus and which originated in the early church. Bultmann's method was simple. He decided what "form" a certain type of story ought to have. If one of the elements in that "form" was missing from one particular story, then that story was "secondary." An example of this procedure is Bultmann's statement that "the stories of the calling of the first disciples from their occupation as fishermen are not actual historical events. They lack entirely any portrayal of adequate motives or historical verisimilitude."[9]

The logic behind this statement seems to be this:

(a) Any author giving a true account of how men became disciples of Jesus would be bound to describe their motives as well as their actions.
(b) The gospel writers do not mention motives, only actions.
(c) Therefore these stories are *not* accounts of historical events.

Clearly it is possible to prove almost any passage to be unhistorical by following this procedure, since the items that must be present for the passage to be regarded as possibly historical have been laid down by the critic in the first place.

---

[8]Ibid., 163.

[9]Rudolf Karl Bultmann, "The New Approach to the Synoptic Problem," in *Existence and Faith: Shorter Writings of Rudolf Bultmann,* trans. Schubert M. Ogden (London: Hodder and Stoughton, 1961; Cleveland/New York: World Publishing Co./Meridian Books, 1960) 53 (USA 47).

Interestingly enough there is a clue to the missing motive in John's gospel. There we are told that Andrew was introduced to Jesus by John the Baptist and brought his brother Simon to meet Jesus also. If Andrew and Simon had previously met Jesus, it is easier to understand why they were willing to leave their jobs and follow him. However, this harmonization of the gospel accounts is not acceptable to many scholars. C. K. Barrett comments that the call of the disciples in Mark's gospel "loses the force it was intended to have if the immediate response of the fishermen and of Levi is given a psychological explanation."[10]

Barrett's interpretation, though different from Bultmann's, is equally dependent on the argument from silence. The logic behind his comment seems to be as follows:

(a) Mark does not provide a psychological explanation for the action of the disciples.
(b) Therefore, according to the law of nonmention, Mark did not believe there was such an explanation.
(c) Therefore John's account, which provides at least a partial explanation, is inconsistent with Mark's.

If we compare the comments of Bultmann and Barrett, we see how adaptable the argument from silence is. Whenever there is an inconsistency between two gospels, it can be used to prove that either of the two is secondary. Let us suppose that Gospel A fails to mention an item that Gospel B mentions. Gospel A is secondary because, had its author had access to primary sources, he would have known this item, and had he known it, he would have been bound to include it. But Gospel B is also secondary. Since Gospel A did not mention this item (and would have been bound to mention it had it been true) the author of Gospel B must have invented it.

(4) *The Acts of the Apostles.* In his *Unity and Diversity in the New Testament*[11] J. D. G. Dunn analyzes the description of the early church in the Acts of the Apostles. One of his tools is the argument from silence. I shall mention two examples of this, not as a criticism of Dunn's book in general, but to illustrate how even a good book can be marred by the use of unsound arguments.

My first example concerns Luke's statement that Paul and Barnabas appointed elders in the Galatian churches (Acts 14:23). Dunn believes this statement to be inaccurate for two reasons:[12]

---

[10]Charles Kingsley Barrett, *The Gospel according to St. John: An Introduction with Commentary and Notes on the Greek Text* (London: S.P.C.K., 1955) 149.

[11]James D. G. Dunn, *Unity and Diversity in the New Testament* (London: SCM Press, 1977).

[12]Ibid., 107, 108.

(a) Elders are nowhere mentioned in Paul's letters to churches. This is literally true (Philippians 1:1 refers to "overseers" not "elders") but irrelevant. If a modern bishop writes a letter to the churches in his diocese and does not mention the clergy, this does not mean there are no clergy in his diocese. It means that he, like Paul, regards the leaders of the church as an integral part of the church, who do not require separate mention in a letter addressed to the church as a whole.

(b) Dunn assumes (rather oddly in the light of his main thesis) that the Galatian churches had an identical form of church organization to that of the church in Antioch. Now Luke's account of the commissioning of Paul and Barnabas in Antioch (Acts 13:1-3) refers to prophets and teachers, but makes no mention of elders. Therefore (according to the law of nonmention) there were no elders at Antioch, and the Galatian churches did not have elders either.

My second example relates to the speeches in Acts. In discussing these speeches Dunn takes the argument from silence a step further, and bases his conclusions not on absolute silence but on relative silence. Luke does include in the speeches some references to the second coming of Christ and the last judgment, but these references are not, in Dunn's opinion, as prominent or as urgent as the references to these matters in the teaching of Jesus. As for "realized eschatology"—the idea that the crisis of the end time is already here—this is "present in 2:15-21 and 3:24, but otherwise wholly absent." From this Dunn draws the "inevitable" conclusion that Luke has "suppressed or ignored" this element in the preaching of the early church.[13]

This is a strange argument. Because a particular idea is mentioned in two speeches, but not mentioned in others, Luke has suppressed or ignored the evidence. His variety is proof of his inconsistency, and his inconsistency is proof of his insincerity.

The argument from relative silence is a potent weapon in the hands of an imaginative critic. It can call into question the accuracy of historians, not only on the grounds that they omit what the critic thinks they should have included, but also on the grounds that what they do include is not expressed as forcefully, or included as often, as the critic thinks it should have been. I do not see how any historian (ancient or modern), or indeed any witness giving evidence in a court of law, could stand against this type of argument. And the difficulties are compounded when a critic is discussing an author who lived 1,900 years ago. How can any modern critic expect to know, with that degree of precision, what an ancient author *should* have written?

---

[13]Ibid., 18, 19.

The Art of Omission

Arguments from silence fail to recognize one simple fact: the art of writing is to a large extent the art of omission. In the preface to his *History of Christian Missions* Stephen Neill remarked that most books on that subject suffered from the attempt at completeness. If all the relevant dates, events, and names are listed, a book becomes unreadable. Against this tendency Neill could see only one safeguard: a resolute determination to omit.[14]

Herman Wouk discovered this when editing his book about the Jewish faith, *This Is My God.* Wouk dropped hundreds of points of information into the notes, and then removed them from the notes. "I have cut and cut again," he writes, "to present the reader with a clear basic outline of this gigantic subject."[15]

In E. H. Carr's judgment the resolute determination to omit is especially important for those writing recent or contemporary history. Whereas students of ancient history have a built-in ignorance because of the scarcity of the sources, modern historians must cultivate this necessary ignorance for themselves. They have the dual task of discovering the few significant facts that are to be turned into facts of history, and of discarding the many insignificant facts as unhistorical.[16]

The authors of the four gospels and Acts faced precisely this situation. They were writing about events in which they or their friends had taken part. Were these events to be recorded in full, then in the words of John's gospel, "the whole world could not contain the books that would be written."[17] They had to omit in order to be readable.

Moreover, books in the ancient world were of limited size. The books of the New Testament were probably first written on papyrus scrolls. Such scrolls were not easy to handle. The writer and the reader had to use both hands, unrolling the scroll with one hand and rolling it up with the other. For this reason a scroll would not normally be much more than thirty feet in length. Bruce Metzger quotes a saying of Callimachus, who catalogued the books in the great library at Alexandria, that "a big book is a big nuisance." The two longest books in the New Testament—Luke and Acts—would each have filled an ordinary papyrus scroll of thirty-one or thirty-two feet.[18]

---

[14]Stephen Charles Neill, *A History of Christian Missions* (Harmondsworth: Penguin Books; Baltimore: Penguin Books Inc., 1964) 9.

[15]Herman Wouk, *This Is My God* (London: Collins, 1976) 267-68.

[16]Edward Hallett Carr, *What Is History?* (Harmondsworth: Penguin Books; New York: Viking Penguin Inc., 1964) 14.

[17]John 21:25.

[18]Bruce Manning Metzger, *The Text of the New Testament* (Oxford: Oxford University Press, 1964) 5, 6.

Papyrus scrolls were also expensive. As Martin Hengel suggests, the early churches may not have been able to afford to buy books, whether of the Old Testament or the New.[19] The gospel writers, we therefore may suppose, would of necessity limit themselves to a single scroll, of a size that could be afforded and easily handled. Onto this scroll they had to condense a three-years record of the life and ministry of Jesus.

The problem they faced is compared by Roland Frye to the problem faced by Shakespeare in portraying the French campaigns of King Henry V. In a chorus Shakespeare apologizes to those who know the real story:

I humbly pray them to admit th' excuse
Of time, of numbers, and due course of things,
Which cannot in their huge and proper life
Be here presented. . . . [20]

As Frye observes, authors and playwrights can never present important events in their "huge and proper life." They are forced by the practical limitations of time and space to use representative persons, incidents, and actions. Referring to his treatment of the battle of Agincourt, Shakespeare writes

. . . —we shall much disgrace
With four or five most vile and ragged foils,
Right ill-dispos'd in brawl ridiculous,
The name of Agincourt. Yet sit and see,
Minding true things by what their mockeries be.[21]

Frye explains that "mockery" is used in its Elizabethan sense of "representation." The selected events represent the "true things" of the original action, but cannot reproduce them in facsimile.[22]

The practical limitations of the playwright are different from those of the author of a book, but in their own way the gospel writers were just as limited for space as Shakespeare. They therefore adopted what is sometimes called the "paradigmatic" style of writing. They did not deal in generalizations, but in vivid selected events which were "paradigms"—particular examples of a general situation.

---

[19]Martin Hengel, *Acts and the History of Earliest Christianity,* trans. John Bowden (London: SCM Press, 1979; Philadelphia: Fortress Press, 1980) 5-8.

[20]*Henry the Fifth,* 5.prologue.3-6.

[21]Ibid., 4.prologue.49-53.

[22]Roland Mushat Frye, "A Literary Perspective for the Criticism of the Gospels," in *Jesus and Man's Hope,* vol. 2 (Perspective 2), ed. Donald G. Miller and Dikran Y. Haddian (Pittsburgh: Pittsburgh Theological Seminary, 1971) 208-10.

According to Martin Hengel, "Luke, with his 'dramatic episodic style' (Haenchen), stood in the broad tradition of Hellenistic historiography which sought to bring historical reality vividly before the eyes of the reader by concentrating on particular paradigmatic events."[23]

In selecting such paradigmatic events one criterion would be the interest factor. Hengel remarks that in ancient history writing what was neglected tended to be everyday life, things that were taken for granted because they were uninteresting. He quotes from Lucian of Samosata's work *How to Write History* (written in the second century C.E.):

> All inessential and minor matters ought to be left on one side, since those who entertain their friends with an opulent meal do not produce salt fish and pea soup at the same time.[24]

Dorothy Sayers saw in this principle the explanation of many "silences" in the gospels. We are twice told that Jesus wept, but never that he smiled. Does this mean he never did smile, and (by the same argument) never said "Please" or "Thank you"? Sayers suggests that these common courtesies may have been left unrecorded precisely because they were common, whereas the tears were "news."[25]

The word "gospel" means "good news," and the gospel writers were "newsmen." People complain today that news bulletins on radio and TV, and news reports in the press, are not an accurate reflection of society: they report the extraordinary rather than the ordinary. But any conveyor of news has to select what is newsworthy and leave out what is not. The gospel writers, like media people today, had to learn the art of selective omission.

The same is true of the epistles. Why is it that Paul, in his summary of the evidence for the resurrection of Jesus (1 Corinthians 15), does *not* mention the empty tomb? Some scholars have argued that he did not mention it because he was not aware of it. This "silence" is then used as evidence to support the theory that the "legend" of the empty tomb was invented by the early church. The trouble with this theory, as Stephen Neill points out, is Paul's statement that Christ was buried and then raised on the third day. This statement, in Neill's words, is "almost unintelligible" apart from a belief in the empty tomb.[26] But even if this were not so, Paul's failure to mention an empty tomb proves nothing about whether or

---

[23]Hengel, *Acts*, 55, 56.

[24]Ibid., 13, 14.

[25]Dorothy Leigh Sayers, *Unpopular Opinions* (London: Victor Gollancz, 1946) 28.

[26]Stephen Charles Neill, *The Interpretation of the New Testament 1861-1961* (London, New York, and Toronto: Oxford University Press, 1964) 287.

not he believed it. All it shows is that Paul, summarizing the evidence for the resurrection of Jesus in about one hundred words, was forced to leave out a lot of
things that—had he the space—he could have included.

It is sometimes assumed that the New Testament writers could have reported
everything they knew, had they only wished to do so, like G. K. Chesterton's
character, Rev. Ellis Shorter. Mr. Shorter was relating an incident at a Dorcas
meeting in his village. Before describing the incident itself, he told in detail of
three other visits he had paid on his way to the meeting, after leaving his house at
11:17 precisely:

> He uttered all this not only with deliberation, but with something that can only
> be called, by a contradictory phrase, eager deliberation. He had, I think, a
> vague memory in his head of the detectives in the detective stories, who al-
> ways sternly require that nothing should be kept back.[27]

The New Testament writers were not in a position to imitate Mr. Shorter. They
could not record every detail that happened, or every word spoken. They summarized. If we ask why they left out some particular thing, which we regard as
important, the answer could lie in a variety of reasons—ignorance, theological
conviction, a sense of what was newsworthy, or simply lack of space. The fact of
omission in itself is not significant, unless we know the reason why. And since
we never do know the reason why, and often have no solid grounds even for
guessing it, it is better to follow the simple rule, "Respect with your own silence
the silence of others."

---

[27]Gilbert Keith Chesterton, *The Club of Queer Trades* (Beaconsfield: Darwen Finlayson, 1960) 61.

The Argument
from Creative Background 5

*To attempt to dissect the Gospels as historical dramas and force the frag-
ments back into earlier forms and stages is like putting Ariel back in the pine
cleft.* —Roland Mushat Frye[1]

The basis of the argument from creative background is the Latin proverb *simulac
hoc, ergo propter hoc,* which may be translated, "everything is the product of its
environment." According to this argument authors are like rivers. Rivers do not
create water, they receive it from springs and streams in their catchment area. In
the same way authors receive their ideas from the streams of thought that are flow-
ing in the corner of the world in which they live. A middle-class Eastern author
will receive middle-class Eastern ideas, a working-class Western author will receive working-class Western ideas. If you want to understand an author's thought,
you have to study the background from which that author came.

In the case of the New Testament this means studying not only the first century in general, but also the various subcultures of the Roman Empire. To understand the Gospel of John we must ask where John got his ideas. Did he borrow
from Jews or from Greeks? Was he a man of Jerusalem or a man of Galilee? Find
out the background, the theory runs, and you have the key to understanding the
text.

This argument applies the rule "we are what we eat" to our minds as well as
to our bodies. It assumes that, just as my body is the product of curry or caviar
(depending on my background), so also my mind is the product of Jewish ideas
or Greek ideas, liberal ideas or conservative ideas (depending on my background). A good illustration of this way of thinking may be found in Dr. Seuss's
story "Scrambled Eggs Super." The storyteller, Peter D. Hooper, is seeking best-
quality eggs for a special dish:

---

[1]Roland Mushat Frye, "A Literary Perspective for the Criticism of the Gospels," in
Jesus and Man's Hope, vol. 2 (Perspective 2), ed. Donald G. Miller and Dikran Y. Hadidian (Pittsburgh: Pittsburgh Theological Seminary, 1971) 212.

I went for the kind that are mellow and sweet
And the world's sweetest eggs are the eggs of the Kweet
Which are due to those very sweet trout which they eat
And those trout . . . well, *they're* sweet 'cause they only eat Blogs
And Blogs, after all, are the world's sweetest frogs
And the reason *they're* sweet is, whenever they lunch
It's always the world's sweetest bees that they munch
And the reason no bees can be sweeter than these . . .
They only eat blossoms off Beezlenut trees
And those Beezlenut blossoms are sweeter than sweet
And that's why I nabbed several eggs from the Kweet.[2]

Peter D. Hooper's methodology has many parallels in modern study of the New Testament.

According to William Beardslee, literary critics over the years have tended to use the model, taken from the natural sciences, of cause and effect. They have tried to explain a literary work by something else, such as the history of the times or the psychological development of the author. However, during the last thirty years many scholars have lost interest in what Beardslee calls "the historical-biographical approach to literature," and have concentrated instead on the literary form and how it works.[3]

This is particularly true in criticism of the parables of Jesus. The aim of older critics, such as C. H. Dodd and Joachim Jeremias, was to find a precise historical background for each parable. Some modern aesthetic critics object that this approach chains the parables to the first century and makes them archaeological artifacts of the past rather than language events of the twentieth century. Comparing these two approaches, Robert Stein sees truth in both sides. We should seek what God is saying to us today through the parables; but we should also remember that the parables were not told in a vacuum: they were parables of *Jesus*. To lose sight of their historical context, Stein asserts, will only lead to misrepresentation and confusion.[4]

The same may be said of all of the New Testament. No author writes in a vacuum. Every generation has its own ideas, which exert more or less influence on everyone who lives in that generation. As the Arab proverb says, men resemble their times more than they resemble their fathers.[5] Knowledge of the background

---

[2]Theodor Seuss Geisel, *The Dr. Seuss Story Book* (London: Collins, 1979) 140.

[3]William A. Beardslee, *Literary Criticism of the New Testament* (Philadelphia: Fortress Press, 1969) 6.

[4]Robert H. Stein, *An Introduction to the Parables of Jesus* (Philadelphia: Westminster Press, 1981) 67.

[5]Marc Bloch, *The Historian's Craft* (Manchester: Manchester University Press, 1954) 35.

of the New Testament is of great value, so long as background remains background.

The difficulties arise when we move from a vague general statement ("every writer is influenced in a general way by his or her background") to particular statements ("Paul, or John, or Jesus borrowed idea X from source Y"). I propose in this chapter to look at some of the problems involved in making this kind of statement.

The Problem of Parallels

Imagine two parallel railway tracks. The engines running along these two tracks have different drivers and different destinations, but they are travelling in the same direction and in the same environment. In the same way, the sayings of Jesus about the kingdom of God or the Son of man are similar, or parallel, to what other people were saying about the kingdom of God and the Son of man in the first century. But can we go further than this and say that Jesus was directly influenced by what any particular person said? What, if anything, follows from the fact that the words or actions of two different people run on parallel tracks?

In *Big Money* P. G. Wodehouse reported the following conversation between Berry Conway and his old servant.

> "Major Flood-Smith," said the Old Retainer, alluding to the retired warrior resident at Castlewood, next door but one, "was doing Swedish exercises in his garden early this morning."
> "Yes?"
> "And the cat at Peacehaven had a sort of fit."
> Berry speculated absently on the mysteries of cause and effect.[6]

As well he might, for the events described could be related to each other in several ways:

(1) *Coincidence*. Major Flood-Smith and the cat acted independently.

(2) *Analogy*. the major and the cat were both influenced by the same electrical currents in the air.

(3) *Genealogy*. one was directly influenced by the other. This could have happened in two ways:

(3a) Major Flood-Smith was influenced by the cat;

(3b) the cat was influenced by Major Flood-Smith.

If there was a direct connection between the two events, (3b) might seem a more probable connection than (3a). But this should not have blinded Berry Con-

---

[6]Pelham Grenville Wodehouse, *Big Money* (London: Herbert Jenkins, 1931) 50.

way's eyes to possibilities (1) and (2). Whenever two reported events or sayings are parallel to each other, all the above possibilities should be considered.

(1) *Coincidence.* In "The Murders in the Rue Morgue" Edgar Allan Poe's detective Arsène Lupin was faced with a coincidence. Money had been received, and three days later the person who received it was murdered. It was commonly assumed that the two events must be causally connected; but in Lupin's opinion coincidences ten times as remarkable as that happened every day. "Coincidences, in general," he declared, "are great stumbling-blocks in the way of that class of thinkers who have been educated to know nothing of the theory of probabilities."[7]

Human nature is the same the world over, and many ideas can be found independently in different cultures. Raymond Panikkar has noted how "there seem to be certain *mythical invariants* in the history of mankind repeated time and time again and appearing in places where historiographical influence is to be excluded."[8] If similar words and ideas occur in different books, we should not be afraid to admit what Marc Bloch called "the innocence of a coincidence." Bloch cited the famous example of the word *bad,* which means the same thing in English and Persian, and commented, "anyone who should pretend to found a connection upon this isolated agreement would sin against the main law of all criticism of coincidences: 'Only large numbers are conclusive'."[9]

(2) *Analogy.* Let us suppose that the resemblances between a book of the New Testament and another document of the same period are too many and too close to be due to coincidence. We then have to ask, in the words of Adolf Deissmann, whether the resemblances are due to analogy or genealogy. Is it a question of two authors sharing a common culture (analogy), or of one author borrowing directly from another (genealogy)?[10]

The Dead Sea Scrolls are a case in point. They were written by members of a monastic community called Essenes, roughly between 135 B.C.E. and 66 C.E. Many of the ideas contained in the scrolls are similar to ideas found in the New Testament. What is the connection between them?

Some have argued for "genealogy"—that John the Baptist belonged to that community, or that John the gospel writer was directly influenced by their teaching. Others have argued for "analogy"—that the writers of the scrolls shared with

---

[7]Edgar Allan Poe, "The Murders in the Rue Morgue," in *The Complete Tales and Poems of Edgar Allan Poe* (New York: The Modern Library, 1938) 160.

[8]Raymond Panikkar, "The Relation of the Gospels to Hindu Culture and Religion," in *Jesus and Man's Hope,* vol. 2 (Perspective 2), ed. Donald G. Miller and Dikran Y. Hadidian (Pittsburgh: Pittsburgh Theological Seminary 1971) 249.

[9]Bloch, *Historian's Craft,* 130-32.

[10]Adolf Deissmann, *Light from the Ancient East,* trans. L. R. M. Strachan (London: Hodder & Stoughton, 1910) 262.

John the Baptist and John the gospel writer ideas that were part of Jewish culture in those days. Martin Hengel, for example, discussing the parallels between Paul's letters and Essene literature, attributes them to the fact that both Essenism and Pharisaism, despite their bitter opposition, went back to a common root in early Judaism, and therefore shared a whole series of theological views.[11]

Another fruitful source of parallels is the prologue to John's gospel. It talks of light, life, birth, sonship, and the word. Ideas such as these can be paralleled in innumerable ancient documents. Robert Kysar has analyzed the "parallels" to John's prologue cited in the two commentaries of Bultmann and Dodd. Of the several hundred parallels adduced, Kysar found the overlap between the commentaries to be only seven percent. In the light of these findings Donald Carson concludes that neither scholar has come close to a comprehensive survey of potential backgrounds.[12]

Most, if not all, of these parallels should be classed as "analogy" rather than "genealogy." They reflect the fact that the New Testament writers lived in the same world and shared the same culture as the authors of the parallel passages. The temptation facing the background investigator is to read more into a parallel than it will bear. In the words of E. E. Ellis, "because of its emphasis on placing Scripture in its historical environment modern biblical scholarship has often tended to convert parallels into influences and influences into sources."[13]

In *Performing Flea* P. G. Wodehouse illustrated what could happen when analogy was confused with genealogy. A tailor claimed that one of the plays of Owen Davis was stolen from a play he (the tailor) had written. Both plays, he alleged, were about a man accused of murder, who turned out in fact to be innocent. When Davis pointed out that many other plays running on Broadway had a similar theme, the tailor replied, "They've *all* stolen my play!"[14]

(3) *Genealogy.* Let us suppose the connection between two writings is so close that there must be a direct link. This raises the further question, Did author A borrow from author B, or author B from author A?

In *The Book of Heroic Failures* is related how Henri Matisse's painting *Le Bateau* was hung upside down in a New York gallery between 17 October and 3

---

[11]Martin Hengel, *Judaism and Hellenism,* vol. 1, trans. John Bowden (London: SCM Press; Philadelphia: Fortress Press, 1974) 254.

[12]Donald A. Carson, *Exegetical Fallacies* (Grand Rapids MI: Baker Book House, 1984) 43, quoting Robert Kysar, "The Background of the Prologue of the Fourth Gospel: A Critique of Historical Methods," *Canadian Journal of Theology* 16 (1970): 250-55.

[13]Edward Earle Ellis, *Paul's Use of the Old Testament* (Grand Rapids MI: Eerdmans; Edinburgh: Oliver & Boyd, 1957) 82.

[14]Pelham Grenville Wodehouse, *Performing Flea* (Harmondsworth: Penguin Books, 1961) 154.

December 1961 without anyone noticing. The painting depicts a sailing boat and summer clouds, with their reflection in the water. The estimated 116,000 visitors who passed through the gallery during that time were unable to distinguish which was the boat and which the reflection.[15]

A similar problem arises when a book of the New Testament closely resembles another document. Which is the original and which is the reflection? Did the New Testament writer borrow from his background, or did the background writer borrow from the New Testament?

This is often difficult to decide. Even when two New Testament books are related to each other, scholars do not agree as to who borrowed from whom. Did Matthew borrow from Mark or Mark from Matthew? Did 2 Peter borrow from Jude or Jude from 2 Peter? When the relationship is between a New Testament book of uncertain date and another book, such as the *Similitudes of Enoch,* of even more uncertain date, the difficulties increase. Every parallel can be explained either way.

In *The Heart of a Goof* P. G. Wodehouse told of the discovery made one day by the golfing enthusiast Wallace Chesney. Until then he had believed that crack players wore plus fours because they were crack players. But suddenly he discovered that the truth was the other way round: they became crack players because they wore plus fours. What he had thought of as a cause was really an effect; what had seemed a source was really a product.[16]

From time to time New Testament scholars make similar discoveries. For example, there are parallels between the ideas of some ancient Greek thinkers called "Gnostics" and certain parts of the New Testament. Some scholars have argued that the writers of the New Testament were influenced by a pre-Christian Gnostic myth that described a heavenly redeemer coming to earth. But other scholars have argued the opposite—that Gnostic ideas about a heavenly redeemer were not the source but the product of Christian teaching about Jesus.

In a book published in 1976 Martin Hengel observed that speculation about pre-Christian Gnosticism showed no desire to come to an end. But in Alexandria, the place where Gnosticism was supposed to have grown up, he could find no evidence for Gnostic speculation prior to Christianity. Hengel comments that "a prime element in history is the chronology of sources. The Gnostic may be forgiven if he does not know either the time or the hour, but not the historian."[17]

Stephen Neill has highlighted the difficulties involved in determining which influence preceded which many centuries ago. He imagined a historian of the

---

[15]Stephen Pile, *The Book of Heroic Failures* (London: Futura Publications, 1980) 134.

[16]Pelham Grenville Wodehouse, *The Heart of a Goof* (London: Herbert Jenkins, 1926) 160.

[17]Martin Hengel, *Jews, Greeks, and Barbarians,* trans. John Bowden (Philadelphia: Fortress Press; London: SCM Press, 1980) 167 n. 66.

twenty-fifth century discovering that, in Sri Lanka in the twentieth century, there existed both a Young Men's Christian Association and a Young Men's Buddhist Association. The historian might well assume that the Buddhist Association was the earlier, since Buddhism had been established in Sri Lanka a lot longer than Christianity. But if he did so, he would be wrong. The Christian association came first, and the idea was borrowed by the Buddhists because it was so successful.[18]

In some cases borrowing can be two-way. In nineteenth-century Britain there was a connection between drunkenness and poverty. G. K. Clark has posed the question, Were people drunken because they were poor, or poor because they were drunken? In the nineteenth century it was commonly assumed that people were poor because they drank too much. In the twentieth century it is often assumed that people drink too much because they are poor. Which assumption is correct?[19]

In such a case there is a two-way influence. Drunkenness is both a source and a product of poverty. The same may be true of the connection between the New Testament and some of its first-century parallels. The mystery religions, for instance, in their rituals and beliefs had some points of similarity with the New Testament. Did the mystery religions borrow from the church, or did the church borrow from the mystery religions, or both? Hard evidence of direct borrowing on either side is difficult to come by.

The Problem of Segregating Cultures

The attempt has sometimes been made to subdivide the ancient world into separate cultural elements—Greek (sometimes called Hellenistic) culture, Jewish culture, and subdivisions of these. If we can find close parallels to a New Testament book in the literature produced in one of these subcultures, then it is often assumed that the writer of that book was influenced by that culture.

The form critics extended this principle to apply not only to the writers of the gospels, but also to the anonymous early Christian storytellers from whom, they believed, those writers got their information. For example, Rudolf Bultmann argued that the miracle stories in the gospels were similar in form to the miracle stories in Hellenistic literature; therefore these stories, as they stand in the gospels, could not have been told by the apostles, who were Palestinian Jews.[20]

---

[18]Stephen Charles Neill, *The Interpretation of the New Testament 1861-1961* (London, New York, and Toronto: Oxford University Press, 1964) 170.

[19]George Sidney Roberts Kitson Clark, *The Critical Historian* (London: Heinemann; New York: Basic Books, 1967) 189.

[20]Rudolf Karl Bultmann, ''The New Approach to the Synoptic Problem,'' in *Existence and Faith: Shorter Writings of Rudolf Bultmann,* trans. Schubert M. Ogden (London: Hodder and Stoughton, 1961) 50.

The problem with this type of argument, as has been increasingly recognized in recent years, is that "Jewish culture" and "Hellenistic culture" were not watertight compartments. The school of life in the first century was not organized in separate classrooms but on an open-plan system. The Dead Sea Scrolls were written by a Jewish community, but contain many ideas that have traditionally been labelled "Hellenistic." Jesus and many of his disciples came from Galilee, an area of mixed Jewish and Greek culture. Paul was a Roman citizen, born in a Greek university city, who studied under a Jerusalem rabbi. Trying to distinguish Jewish and Greek elements in a first-century document is like trying to taste the separate ingredients when eating a cake. You can be sure a particular ingredient is there, but you cannot be sure in what proportion it is combined with the other ingredients. And you certainly cannot work out, from the presence of a particular ingredient, who baked the cake.

In his book *Judaism and Hellenism* Martin Hengel has reexamined the familiar distinction between Hellenistic and Palestinian Judaism. In Hengel's opinion, from about the middle of the third century B.C.E. all Judaism should be designated "Hellenistic Judaism," including that of the mother country. He works out his thesis at various levels.[21]

(1) At the social and economic level, Hengel reminds us that, by the time of Jesus, Palestine had already been under Hellenistic rule for some 360 years, and virtually every inhabitant of Palestine came into contact with the new masters. The parables of Jesus, with their great landowners, tax farmers, administrators, moneylenders, day laborers, and customs officials, with speculation in grain, slavery for debt, and the leasing of land, reflect the economic conditions brought about by Hellenism.[22]

(2) At the level of language, there was certainly a significant difference between those whose mother tongue was Greek and those whose mother tongue was Aramaic. But from the second century B.C.E. onwards Jerusalem was an international city, the spiritual center of a world Judaism. As Greek inscriptions show, Jerusalem must have had a considerable minority who spoke Greek as their mother tongue. Galilee also had for a long time special links with the Phoenician cities, and two of the Galilean disciples, Andrew and Philip, had Greek names.[23]

(3) At the intellectual level, even those Jews who were most committted to the Torah were subject to the influence of ideas such as natural revelation, retribution after death and a future realm of peace, spirits of the dead, astrology, man-

---

[21]Martin Hengel, *Judaism and Hellenism,* vol. 1, trans. John Bowden (London: SCM Press; Philadelphia: Fortress Press, 1974) 104.

[22]Ibid., 1, 56.

[23]Ibid., 104.

ticism, and magic. "Jewish Palestine," Hengel concludes, "was no hermetically sealed island in the sea of Hellenistic oriental syncretism."[24]

Any scholar seeking to classify the ideas of particular cultures or subcultures would do well to remember the words of Edward de Bono:

> Much of the difficulty with classifying is that the mind prefers static definitions. We talk of "grey" as a definite classification, not just a stage in the dynamic process of black becoming white. The difference between a static and a dynamic definition is that the latter is not really a definition at all, but merely a possibility.[25]

Moreover, we must not forget that Jesus and the New Testament writers were creative thinkers, and creative thinkers have always been able to combine various elements in the culture of their day. The great composer Handel, in the judgment of Sir Thomas Beecham, wrote Italian music better than any Italian, French music better than any Frenchman, English music better than any Englishman, and, with the exception of Bach, outrivalled all other Germans.[26] It would have been interesting to read Beecham's reaction to the views of a musical form critic who argued that, since Handel was German born, any of his music written in an Italian style must be the work of a later editor.

The Problem of Limited Knowledge

We saw earlier that theories about the composition of the New Testament are difficult to test because of our limited knowledge of the period. This is especially true of theories that link author A with background B. To establish a direct link between a New Testament author and his supposed background you need to show, not only that the author's ideas fit that situation, but also that they would not fit so well any other situation. Our knowledge of the period is too limited to make this possible. Even if it can be shown that a New Testament book fits background B better than any other known background, it could still belong to background C, a circle of ideas that happens not to be mentioned in the documents that happen to have survived.

According to Martin Hengel, "the basic problem in writing a history of early Christianity lies in the fragmentariness of the sources and the haphazard way in

---

[24]Ibid., 311-12.

[25]Edward de Bono, *The Use of Lateral Thinking* (London: Penguin Books, 1971) 87.

[26]Sir Thomas Beecham, in an essay introducing a recording of Handel's *Messiah*, record set GL 02444(3) (London: RCA Records, 1977).

which they have survived."[27] Every time a new document is discovered, it not only adds to our knowledge of the period, but often also reveals how inaccurate were the guesses about life during that period that were made before the discovery.

A striking illustration of this is the Greek language in which the New Testament was written. Many nineteenth-century scholars, noting the contrast between the language of the New Testament and the language of most ancient Greek literature, believed the New Testament was written in a special "Christian Greek." At the end of the nineteenth century, however, a mass of ancient documents was discovered in Egypt, written on papyrus. Some were private letters, written in colloquial style by people of little education. Again and again words and phrases from the New Testament appeared in these letters, and it became clear that the New Testament was written, not in "Christian Greek," but in the popular nonliterary Greek of that time.

The "Christian Greek" hypothesis is now past history; but although that particular mistake will not be made again, the same type of mistake can be made at any time. We can fail to allow for that element in the background to the New Testament that the patchiness of our sources hides from our eyes. New discoveries (such as the discovery of the Egyptian papyri or of the Dead Sea Scrolls) increase our knowledge of the ancient world; but a patchwork quilt remains patchy even after a new patch has been added.

Imagine a twenty-fifth century scholar whose knowledge of twentieth-century British journalism is confined to some copies of *The Times* that have survived. One day he learns of some copies of *The Sun*, which have been discovered by an archaeologist. This would be a very exciting find, and would greatly increase that scholar's knowledge of the twentieth century. But it might also lead him to forget how patchy that knowledge still was—that there were many aspects of twentieth-century British journalism not covered by the two types of literature that happened to survive. He would need to resist the temptation to regard every new journalistic fragment that came to light as a product either of *Times*-culture or of *Sun*-culture.

Premature pigeonholing is a constant temptation for students of the New Testament. One reason for this is the continuing influence of the nineteeth-century scholar F. C. Baur. In the judgment of W. G. Kümmel, one of Baur's lasting contributions to New Testament research was the perception that "the task of historical criticism of the New Testament is only fulfilled when the historical place of origin of a writing within the framework of early Christian history is also estab-

---

[27]Martin Hengel, *Acts and the History of Earliest Christianity*, trans. John Bowden (London: SCM Press, 1979; Philadelphia: Fortress Press, 1980) 5.

lished.''[28] But suppose we do not know enough to establish the historical place of origin of a New Testament book? Scholars of earlier centuries were content to be ignorant; but followers of Baur, who believe that the background is the message, feel compelled to reconstruct the origin of every book, and of every subsection of that book—by guesswork if necessary—since without such a reconstruction the book is unintelligible. Guesswork, even when it goes by the name of inductive method, is not the best form of scholarship. It may turn out that scholars of the "precritical" era, who believed with Socrates that the beginning of wisdom was to admit ignorance, were more scientific than their less-inhibited successors.

One tool of the premature pigeonholer is the *argumentum ex noto* (argument from source availability). According to this argument we must try to understand the New Testament in the light of that small part of its background that is known to us. It is better to guess on the basis of what we know than to sit on the fence because of what we do not know.

A good example of the *argumentum ex noto* is F. W. Beare's attempt to date 1 Peter in the time of Pliny. Pliny was governor of two provinces in the region south of the Black Sea to which 1 Peter was addressed. He wrote to the emperor Trajan for advice on how to deal with Christians. Trajan advised him to continue his existing policy; he was not to seek Christians out, but should execute them if they were accused by other people, and refused to worship the Roman gods. Beare comments that

> Pliny's description of his experience and methods could not conceivably correspond more closely to the words of 1 Peter 4:12-16; and there is certainly nothing resembling it to be found elsewhere in ancient literature or in official documents. It would therefore seem unnecessary to look further for the persecution which called forth our letter, and we may make the tentative conjecture that it was written at or about the same time as Pliny's letter to Trajan, i.e., A.D. 111–112.[29]

This argument reminds me of the man who entered a large railroad station to catch a train. There was only one train immediately visible—an express train, corresponding in all respects to the type of train he needed to catch. It therefore seemed unnecessary to look further for his train and he climbed in. Only when the train was leaving the station did he notice other express trains, in parts of the station he

---

[28]Werner Georg Kümmel, *The New Testament: The History of the Investigation of Its Problems,* trans. S. McLean Gilmour and Howard C. Kee (London: SCM Press; Nashville/New York: Abingdon Press, 1972) 131.

[29]Francis Wright Beare, *The First Epistle of Peter,* 2nd ed. (Oxford: Basil Blackwell, 1961) 14.

had not discovered, and realize that the train in which he was travelling was going in the wrong direction.

Other Roman governors, in the days of Nero and Domitian, may have written letters describing how they dealt with Christians. If so, their letters have so far not been discovered. It so happens that Pliny's letters have survived. A theory like Beare's, which picks the best background from those available at the time of writing, may last only until the discoveries of the next generation.

The Problem of Reconstructing "Life Situations"

The most striking form of the *argumentum ex noto* in the twentieth century has been the attempt to reconstruct the "life situation" (in German, *Sitz im Leben*) of every saying and every story in the gospels—both the situations in the ministry of Jesus in which his teaching was originally given, and the situations in the life of the early church in which that teaching was handed down.

This is an attractive task, because it gives scope to the imagination. As an art form, it bears some resemblance to the writing of historical novels, in which the author's imagination helps the past to come alive. But as a tool of scientific scholarship it leaves much to be desired.

So far as "life situations" within the ministry of Jesus are concerned, these are often provided for us by the gospel writers. Scholars vary in their estimate of these. Some regard them with respect, as providing a reliable framework for the ministry of Jesus. Others are more skeptical; their faith in their own ability to reconstruct the "life situations" of Jesus is greater than their faith in the ability of the gospel writers to do the same thing.

The logic behind this selective skepticism is curious. We are told that the gospels are very unreliable: the most they can tell us is what the early church believed, not what Jesus actually said and did. But apart from the gospels we have virtually no information about the life of Jesus and the situations he faced. It follows that the "life situation" attributed to a particular parable or saying, unless it is purely a figment of someone's imagination, must be taken from the stock of "life situations" described in the gospels. This inevitably raises the question, Can reliable speculation be based on unreliable evidence?

It is no wonder some skeptical scholars reject this whole approach. John Drury, for example, when discussing the parable of the sower and its interpretation (Mark 4:10-20), does not ask which parts go back to Jesus and which were added by the early church. He sees the whole section as a literary unity. The parable must be regarded as a parable of Mark's, which "may be Jesus' too by some undiscoverable route of tradition—we cannot tell."[30] Not everyone will share Drury's skepticism, but it is at least consistent.

---

[30]John H. Drury, *The Parables in the Gospels* (London: SPCK, 1985) 55.

Even more speculative than the search for situations in the life of Jesus is the search for situations in the life of the early church. To argue from hypothetical "life situations" in the early church is to use, not the *argumentum ex noto*, but the *argumentum ex ignoto*—an argument based, not on the availability of sources, but on the availability of modern imaginative reconstructions.

It is easy to imagine situations in the life of the early church to which the sayings of Jesus would be relevant. The problem is that so much of his teaching would be relevant to more than one situation. Stephen Neill has illustrated this from the story of Jesus blessing the children. In what situations, Neill asks, was this story told in the early church? Was it told in connection with infant baptism? Was it told in discussions about the children of mixed marriages, where only one parent was a Christian? Was it told to counteract the neglect of children in the Roman Empire? Was it told in sermons to teach the lesson of childlike faith? It could have been told in all of these situations, and in others as well. Neill criticizes those who simply assume the story was connected with infant baptism, and comments that "to treat a possibility as if it were a probability, and then a little later to treat it as though it were a certainty, is an offence against the basic canons of critical and scientific work."[31]

At first sight, it may not seem to matter whether scholars have guessed a "life situation" right or wrong. The problem arises if they go a step further and argue that, because one of the gospel sayings fits into a supposed situation within the early church, it was the church community that constructed the saying. Such an argument is suspect for two reasons.

First, as I have already said, we do not know enough about the early Christian communities to warrant judgments of this sort. Martin Hengel comments on these so-called "community constructions" that we know far less about the "communities" which are said to have given rise to such traditions than we do about Jesus himself. These "community constructions" often seem, in Hengel's judgment, to be modern fabrications rather than historical realities.[32]

Second, gospel sayings that can be shown to be appropriate to situations in the early church would in many cases be equally appropriate to situations in the life of Jesus. It is left to the whim of the scholar concerned whether a particular saying is credited to Jesus or to the early church.

Let me illustrate this from Norman Perrin's book *Rediscovering the Teaching of Jesus*. Perrin refers to a number of sayings in the New Testament, including two in the gospels, of the form "if anyone does X, God will do X to him." According to Ernst Käsemann, early Christian prophets were in the habit of making

---

[31]Neill, *Interpretation*, 248.

[32]Hengel, *Acts*, 25.

pronouncements of this kind, especially at celebrations of the Eucharist. Perrin accepts Käsemann's argument and claims that, if these sayings fit into this "life situation" within the early church, they cannot fit into the life situation of Jesus. They may ultimately be based on something Jesus said, but, in Perrin's view, they are a *direct* source for knowledge of early Christian prophecy, not of the teaching of Jesus.[33]

I wonder if there is any other area of scholarship, apart from study of the Bible, where this kind of argument would be taken seriously. There is no reason to doubt that early Christian prophets made pronouncements of this nature. But this form of speaking was not invented by them. It goes back at least to the Old Testament, to sayings like 1 Samuel 2:20: "those who honor me I will honor, and those who despise me will be lightly esteemed." Jesus, who was among other things a first-century prophet, could have used this form of speech just as easily as prophets in the early church. You cannot deduce the background of a saying from the form of the words it embodies.

In an article entitled "On Using the Wrong Tool," M. D. Hooker has examined the tools used by scholars to locate gospel sayings either in the ministry of Jesus or in the life of the early church. The tools consist of various criteria for testing the genuineness of sayings. A saying is not likely to be genuine if it reflects what the early church believed, or what the writer of the gospel believed. A saying is likely to be genuine if it can be easily translated back into Aramaic, or if it is similar to other sayings the critic believes to be genuine. Tests such as these, Hooker suggests, are too imprecise to prove anything:

> In the end, the answers which the New Testament scholar gives are not a result of applying objective tests and using precision tools, they are very largely the result of his own presuppositions and prejudices.[34]

Modern reconstructions of "life situations" tend to follow the jigsaw theory. If two pieces in a jigsaw match each other in color and shape, one may assume they belong together. In the same way, if a story or saying in the gospels seems to match up with a situation in the life of Jesus or in the life of the early church, adherents of the jigsaw theory assume they belong together and join them up.

The problem with the jigsaw theory is this: a jigsaw puzzle has a limited number of pieces and therefore a limited number of possible color-and-shape combinations. But in real life there is no limit to the number of ways things might have

---

[33]Norman Perrin, *Rediscovering the Teaching of Jesus* (London: SCM Press, 1967) 22, referring to Ernst Käsemann, "Sentences of Holy Law in the New Testament," in *New Testament Questions of Today,* trans. W. J. Montague and Wilfred F. Bunge (London: SCM Press; Philadelphia: Fortress Press, 1969) 66-81, cf. esp. 77-78.

[34]Morna Dorothy Hooker, "On Using the Wrong Tool," *Theology* 35 (1972): 581.

happened. In E. H. Carr's words, "History has been called an enormous jigsaw with a lot of missing parts."[35]

This is particularly true of the period of the New Testament. If the public ministry of Jesus lasted for three years, or roughly a thousand days, he must have faced many thousands of life situations, only a handful of which are recorded in the gospels. With regard to life situations in the early church, the case is even worse. What did it really feel like to share in a first-century baptism service at Antioch, or a prayer meeting at Rome? To answer such a question we need a vivid imagination and a willingness to guess.

The attempt to provide a specific "life situation" for a particular story or saying is, of course, more speculative than the attempt to provide a general type of "life situation" for a general category of stories or sayings. Erhardt Güttgemanns suggests that the concept of *Sitz im Leben* should properly be used only in the latter sense, and his translator W. G. Doty renders the phrase accordingly as "sociological setting." But even in this generalized sense Güttgemanns finds the idea highly speculative.[36] He is critical of sociological surveys of New Testament times, such as Martin Dibelius's account of how primitive Galilean Christianity was transformed in the Hellenistic world. This strikes him as rather hypothetical, since we know very little about the sociological structure of the early churches beyond general references to Galilean fishermen and passages such as 1 Corinthians 1:26-31. In Güttgemanns's opinion, "it would be best not to sketch whole historical canvases on the bases of conjectures alone."[37]

George Eliot once described a conversation in an inn on the origins of Presbyterianism. Mr. Luke Byles had stated that Presbyterianism was derived from the word "presbyter," meaning an elder. Mr. Dempster disagreed:

> "Don't contradict *me*, sir," stormed Dempster. " . . . I say the word 'presbyterian' derived from John Presbyter, a miserable fanatic who wore a suit of leather, and went from town to village, and from village to hamlet, inoculating the vulgar with the asinine virus of Dissent."
>
> "Come, Byles, that seems a good deal more likely," said Mr. Tomlinson, in a conciliatory tone, apparently of opinion that history was a process of ingenious guessing.[38]

---

[35]Edward Hallett Carr, *What Is History?* (Harmondsworth: Penguin Books; New York: Viking Penguin Inc., 1964) 13.

[36]Erhardt Güttgemanns, *Candid Questions Concerning Gospel Form Criticism,* trans. William G. Doty (Pittsburgh: Pickwick Press, 1979) 259.

[37]Ibid., 55.

[38]George Eliot, *Scenes of Clerical Life* (Oxford: Clarendon Press, 1985) 192.

Mr. Tomlinson's approach to history is not dead. Ingenious guessing is the basis of a good many attempts to reconstruct the ''life situation'' of books, or passages in books, written many centuries ago. These attempts are only plausible because, in the absence of firm evidence to support them, there is likewise no firm evidence to refute them.

Scholars seeking to be amateur detectives and to reconstruct the events of the first century would do well to remember the words addressed to Superintendent Parker by Lord Peter Wimsey:

> "Go on with your theory—only do remember that to guess how a job *might* have been done isn't the same thing as proving that it *was* done that way. If you will allow me to say so, that is a distinction which people of your profession are very liable to overlook."[39]

The Problem of Originality

The twentieth-century search for the source material of the gospels is partly a historical search—an attempt to write what Bultmann called a history of the synoptic tradition. But it is also a theological search—an attempt to understand such ideas as the kingdom of God and the Son of man in the light of their usage in the literature of the period. This attempt has a real but limited value. Jesus and the apostles did make use of current ideas; but they were also original thinkers, and what they meant by these ideas cannot be simply deduced from contemporary usage.

Originality is not independence, but creative dependence. Andrew Hacker illustrates this from the writings of Karl Marx. He records a long list of the sources quoted in *The Communist Manifesto,* which led one commentator to the judgment that ''Marx is as little the originator of socialism and communism as the chairman of General Motors Corporation is the inventor of the automobile.'' Hacker agrees that theorists can never be shown to have originated any of their ideas; the importance of Marx was that he took the thoughts of others and integrated them in a new and persuasive way.[40]

The gospel writers, like Marx, were creative borrowers. Authors who borrow creatively—whether from specific sources, or from the general climate of thought in their day—make the material they borrow their own. It becomes, in a sense, just as much their own as the comments they add themselves. And those com-

---

[39]Dorothy Leigh Sayers, *Busman's Honeymoon* (London: Victor Gollancz, 1972) 262.

[40]Andrew Hacker, *Political Theory: Philosophy, Ideology, Science* (New York: Macmillan, 1961) 15.

ments in their turn are based on experiences they have gained over the years, on people they have talked to, on sources in their subconscious mind. If we try to isolate specific sources in any author's work, or to separate source from commentary, the danger is that we may cease, in Dan Via's words, to "apprehend the text as a whole or a totality."[41]

Via sees this as a special danger for those redaction critics who split a gospel into tradition and redaction, and say that the differences between the two must be allowed to stand in their tension. He quotes as an example Georg Strecker's statement that Mark was interested, not in the atoning significance of Jesus' death, but in the fact of it; if one wants to find Jesus' death interpreted as atoning in Mark, one must look to preredactional elements (such as 14:24).

> Thus in true redaction-critical fashion Strecker separates fact from interpretation, sets them over against each other as unrelated, and attributes them to two different theologies—all of this, incredibly, despite the fact that both belong to the same *story*.[42]

The originality of original thinkers does not consist only in their ability to integrate borrowed materials; they are also able to create what was not there before. When Gordon Rupp was accused of portraying, in the *Cambridge Modern History,* a Luther who had come straight down out of heaven, he replied that so Luther did. "The exciting thing about human beings," he continued, "and a reason for the historical study of great men, is to seek the 'X' in their equation, the point at which they cease to be explained by heredity and environment and the thought world of their contemporaries."[43]

What is true of Luther is much more true of Jesus. Jesus was not just a borrower, he was an inspired artist in his use of words. The only way to discover what he meant by phrases such as "Son of man" is to sit at his feet and study what he said. If we find that his use of this phrase was more varied than its use in any other document of the period, that should not surprise us.

In his 1949 essay entitled "The Creative Element in the Thought of Jesus," Vincent Taylor lodged a protest against the assumption that "if we know all there is to know about the history of the idea of the Son of Man, of the Messiah, and the Suffering Servant, we know what Jesus thought." In fact, Taylor declared, we know nothing of the kind.

---

[41]Dan Otto Via, Jr., *Kerygma and Comedy in the New Testament* (Philadelphia: Fortress Press, 1975) 72.

[42]Ibid., 73, referring to Georg Strecker, "The Passion and Resurrection Predictions in Mark's Gospel," *Interpretation* 22 (1968): 440.

[43]Gordon Rupp, *Just Men* (London: Epworth Press, 1977) 33.

Genius borrows, but it also transmutes; it leaves nothing as it finds it, but prints upon all an original stamp. . . . Schweitzers are always needed to tell us that Jesus is the great Unknown, a stranger to our generation and its ways of thinking, and yet is the most modern of all because in His hands are the keys of life and of death.[44]

Jesus and the apostles were not related to their background as a chicken is related to an egg. They were the creative agents of a creative God. The New Testament is not a mechanical response to external influences; it is the record of people inspired by God to see new things, and to see old things in a new way.

[44]Vincent Taylor, "The Creative Element in the Thought of Jesus," in *New Testament Essays* (London: Epworth Press, 1970) 40.

The Argument
from Consistency

6

"Ah," said Poirot, "the conflicting statements! Yes, one always has them."

"And what a nuisance they are to clear up, too," said the inspector. "Sometimes they matter but in nine times out of ten they don't."[1]

The argument from consistency assumes than an author always uses the same style of writing, and a preacher always uses the same style of preaching. To discover whether one of the Pauline letters was really written by Paul, you compare it with Paul's other letters. To discover whether a saying attributed to Jesus was really uttered by Jesus, you compare it with his other sayings. Only if the style is the same as elsewhere can the letter or the saying be genuine.

There are thirteen letters bearing Paul's name in the New Testament. They are written in several different styles—the argumentative style of the letter to the Romans, the meditative style of the letter to the Ephesians, the practical style of the letters to Timothy and Titus. According to the argument from consistency, Paul must have written all his letters in one consistent style; the critic's task is to discover which of these styles is the genuine Paul.

One present-day advantage of this argument is that it can be computerized. With the help of a computer, Andrew Q. Morton has analyzed the number of times certain Greek words occur in the letters bearing Paul's name. In Morton's opinion these computer findings prove that Paul wrote only five of the thirteen letters, and the other eight were written by persons unknown.[2] Other critics have reached similar conclusions, not by using a computer, but by a kind of computer mentality—the mechanical use of tables of statistics to prove what an author could or could not have written.

---

[1]Agatha Christie, *Dead Man's Folly* (London: Collins, 1973) 157.

[2]Andrew Queen Morton and James McLeman, *Christianity and the Computer* (London: Hodder & Stoughton, 1964) 32.

The problem with computerized criticism, as Harvey K. McArthur has pointed out, is that "while the computer can count, it is the responsibility of the critic to determine what it should count and how the results should be evaluated."[3] Critics in fact differ greatly in their judgment as to the authorship of the thirteen "Pauline" letters. Some think Paul wrote all thirteen; others that he wrote all except the letters to Timothy and Titus; others that he wrote all but the letters to Timothy, Titus, and the Ephesians; others that he wrote all but the letters to Timothy, Titus, the Ephesians, and the Colossians; and so on. Virtually all these critics give statistics about the words used in the various letters. They differ in their conclusions not because their statistics vary, or because their computers are unreliable, but because they make different assumptions, and therefore interpret the same statistics differently.

A similar situation arises in gospel criticism. The gospels record Jesus teaching in a wide variety of styles. Do we attribute this to the versatility of Jesus, or to the inconsistency of the gospel writers? In other words, how far should we expect a preacher or an author to be consistent? It seems to me that, before a charge of inconsistency is laid, there are seven factors to be taken into consideration.

Authors and Preachers Are Human

Agatha Christie once described how a group of people, including a retired solicitor, Mr. Treves, were discussing a recent legal case:

> "I was thinking," said Mr. Treves, "not so much of the various points of law raised—though they were interesting—very interesting. . . . I was thinking, as I say, not of the points of law but of the—well, of the *people* in the case."
>
> Everybody looked rather astonished. They had considered the people in the case only as regarding their credibility or otherwise as witnesses.[4]

Any professional group can fall into the same trap: they can come to regard other people as sources of correct or incorrect information, rather than as human beings. This is certainly true of New Testament scholars. They can easily forget that the authors of the New Testament books were human; and no human being is totally consistent. The fact that an author's writing is uneven, with some purple passages and some off-white passages, may prove nothing except the author's humanity.

One inconsistent author was William Shakespeare. Some critics have used the inconsistencies in Shakespeare as a basis for dividing up his plays into genuine

---

[3]Harvey K. McArthur, "Computer Criticism," *Expository Times* 76 (1964/1965): 368.

[4]Agatha Christie, *Towards Zero* (London: Pan Books Ltd., 1948) 8.

and nongenuine sections. The snags in this approach were exposed many years ago in an article entitled "The Disintegration of Shakespeare" by E. K. Chambers.[5] Chambers's argument is worth summarizing, since the critical method of J. M. Robertson, which Chambers was attacking, has often been applied in study of the New Testament.

According to Chambers there were three stages in Robertson's approach. First came impressionist judgments—some plays, or parts of plays, repelled him because of clumsy stagecraft or false sentiment or the like. These judgments were then confirmed by stylistic tests, largely related to the chronological phases of Shakespeare's blank verse. Finally came the search for clues to the presence of alien hands, such as words rare in Shakespeare's vocabulary but traceable in the writings of other authors.[6]

This procedure, in Chambers's opinion, rested on a false view of Shakespeare. It regarded him, not as a human being, but as a superhuman figure, whose genius must always be consistent. There are pedestrian passages in Shakespeare, there are inconsistencies of narrative and time sequence. These do not create the same problem on the stage as they do for the student poring over the printed text in his or her study. Chambers concludes:

> I come to accept Shakespeare, not to praise him. Obviously there are things in the plays which any other Elizabethan could just as well, or just as badly have written. They do not perturb me, as they perturb Mr. Robertson, to the point of searching for clues to another man.[7]

We should bear Chambers's remarks in mind when discussing, for example, whether Paul could have written the Pastoral Epistles. These epistles do not exhibit the same verve and enthusiasm as Paul's letters to churches. But human beings are not machines. Two works by the same author are like two children of different ages born to the same parents. In some cases the family likeness is obvious. In other cases no one would know, to look at them, that they were related. In the same way literary works reflect the complexity of the authors who gave them birth.

When Sir Arthur Conan Doyle was producing the stage version of *The Speckled Band,* they had a live boa to play the title role, a snake which was the pride of his heart. Doyle was therefore disgusted when the critic of the *Daily Telegraph* ended his disparaging review with the words, "The crisis of the play was produced by the appearance of a palpably artificial serpent." But one can understand

---

[5]Edmund Kerchever Chambers, *Shakespearean Gleanings* (London: Oxford University Press, 1944) 1-21.

[6]Ibid., 5, 6.

[7]Ibid., 8, 9.

the critic's mistake. A real snake, having a personality of its own, would not be as consistently snake-like as an artificial snake. Critics in search of consistency tend to prefer the artificial to the real.[8]

Consistency is a characteristic, not of animals and vegetables, but of minerals. One reason mass producers of cars prefer robots to people is that robots are more consistent. Had the New Testament been written by robots, it would have been consistent enough to satisfy any critic and any computer.

Authors and Preachers Are Paradoxical

The New Testament writers were happy to use words inconsistently, not only in different letters, but even within the same letter. Paul declared that he was perfect (Philippians 3:15) and not perfect (Philippians 3:12). John believed Christians may commit sin (1 John 2:1) and that they do not commit sin (1 John 3:9). These authors used words as a composer uses a musical instrument, taking advantage of its full range, and where necessary making creative use of discord.

This is not always recognized in the statistical approach. For example, one argument used in support of the proposition that Paul did not write Ephesians is that some words used in that letter were used elsewhere by Paul in a different sense. This argument has been rightly criticized by Henry Chadwick. The words in question, he declares, lend themselves to ambiguity, and may be termed "balloon-words," capable of inflation to a varied degree in accordance with the necessities of the moment.[9]

A good example of a balloon-word may be found in the parable of the Good Samaritan. This parable, as Luke records it, was told in answer to the question, "Who is my neighbor?"—that is to say, Who is the neighbor whom, according to the Old Testament law, I should love as myself? But the parable ends with the question, "Who was neighbor to the man who fell among thieves?" Commentators have often noted that, in response to a question regarding a neighbor as an object, Jesus poses a question in which the neighbor is a subject, and have suggested various reasons why Jesus should have done this.

But John D. Crossan does not believe in balloon-words. The important thing for Crossan is that the two uses of the word "neighbor" are inconsistent. The parable of Luke 10:30-35 would fit quite well with 10:27-29 showing that the neighbor is anyone in need; and it would also fit well with 10:36 indicating that the

---

[8]Arthur Conan Doyle, *The Final Adventures of Sherlock Holmes* (London: W. H. Allen, 1981) 39, 40.

[9]Henry Chadwick, "Ephesians," in *Peake's Commentary on the Bible,* ed. Matthew Black (Sunbury-on-Thames: Thomas Nelson & Sons Ltd., 1962) 982.

neighbor is the one who assists another's need; but it cannot, in Crossan's opinion, go with both 10:27-29 and 10:36 simultaneously. Accordingly, he divides up the story in Luke into two sections, one of which goes back to Jesus, and one of which was added by the early church.[10]

This idea that a word can have only one meaning is not confined to New Testament scholars. Richmal Crompton's eleven-year-old hero William expressed the same sentiment when discussing the Nazis with his friends.

"What did you say they were called?" said William.

"Nasties," replied Henry, who as usual was the fount of information on the subject.

"They can't be called nasties," said William. "No one would call themselves a name like that. That mus' be what people call them that don't like them."

"No, it's their real name," persisted Henry. "They really are called nasties. Nasty means something quite different in Germany."

"Don't be silly," said William. "Nasty couldn't mean anything but nasty anywhere. . . . "[11]

Authors and Preachers Repeat Themselves with Variations

The argument from consistency does not only assume that Jesus and the apostles spoke and wrote in a single uniform style; it also assumes that, when they used a metaphor or figure of speech, they always used it in the same way, to make the same point. If the gospels record that Jesus used a particular metaphor in two different contexts to make two different points, then one or the other gospel must be in error. The principle was clearly stated by C. H. Dodd.

. . . sometimes a parable occurs in two or more Gospels with different and even inconsistent applications, as, for example, the parable of the Savourless Salt. We must suppose that Jesus intended some one definite application; hence either one, or more probably both, of the applications are secondary.[12]

One wonders on what grounds we "must suppose" that Jesus could not have used the metaphor of salt losing its savor in two different contexts to make two

---

[10]John Dominic Crossan, *In Parables* (San Francisco and New York: Harper & Row, 1973) 59, 60.

[11]Richmal Crompton, *William the Detective* (London: Collins, 1971) 85.

[12]Charles Harold Dodd, *The Parables of the Kingdom,* rev. ed. (London: Collins; New York: Charles Scribner's Sons, 1961) 25-26 (British ed.), 16-17 (USA ed.). (The pagination in the USA edition differs from that of the British.)

different points if he so wished. Dorothy Sayers, in the composition of her radio plays on the life of Christ, worked on a quite different principle. When distributing the parables and sayings over the various plays, she realized that some would not be in their original context. But she also believed that Jesus, having thought of such good stories as the Good Samaritan and the Prodigal Son, would have been foolish to confine them to a single audience. He would repeat them over and over, till his disciples knew them by heart in all their variations.[13]

Accordingly, when faced with "doublets," such as the parable of the Talents in Matthew and the parable of the Pounds in Luke, Sayers regarded them as the same basic story, varied by Jesus to suit the occasion. She found a parallel to this procedure in Appasamy and Streeter's description of the practice of "another Oriental teacher"—Sadhu Sundar Singh:

> The Sadhu's mind is an overflowing reservoir of anecdote, illustration, epigram, and parable, but he never makes the slightest effort to avoid repetition; in fact he appears to delight in it. "We do not," he says, "refuse to give bread to hungry people because we have already given bread to others." Hence we have constantly found the same material occurring in more than one of the written or printed authorities we have used. "My mouth," he says, "has no copyright"; and many sayings that we had noted down from his own lips we afterwards discovered to be already in print. In most cases the versions differ extraordinarily little, but we have always felt free to correct or supplement one version by another at our own discretion.[14]

The quest for the original version of the parables and sayings of Jesus has been greatly influenced by a twentieth-century dogma called "the law of non-repetition." According to this law Jesus can only have spoken once about any one subject. If the gospel writers record various sayings on a particular subject, only one of these can be original.

A typical example of this law in operation is T. W. Manson's discussion of the sayings of Jesus about divorce and remarriage. Manson listed four sayings—two from Matthew, one from Mark, and one from Luke. After discussing the four sayings, he concluded that one of them was "the original," and the others were either expansions or misunderstandings of the original by the early church. Manson did not consider the possibility that Jesus spoke on various occasions about this subject, so that the variations in the gospels reflected the variety in Jesus' own teaching.[15]

---

[13]Dorothy Leigh Sayers, *The Man Born to Be King* (London: Victor Gollancz, 1943) 32.

[14]Ibid., n.1, quoting Burnett Hillman Streeter and Aiyadurai Jesudasen Appasamy, *The Sadhu* (London: Macmillan, 1921), the USA edition of which was entitled *The Message of Sadhu Sundar Singh* (New York: Macmillan, 1921).

[15]Thomas Walter Manson, *The Sayings of Jesus* (London: SCM Press, 1949) 136-38.

Manson's approach (which is still widely adopted) was based on a false methodology. He was examining reports of the oral teaching of a travelling preacher, but his methods were borrowed from the textual criticism of written manuscripts. It is easy to imagine how this methodology arose. When the modern search for the prehistory of the gospel sayings began, there were no rules in existence as to how to conduct it. It must have been tempting simply to take over the existing rules for textual criticism and apply them to the teaching of Jesus.

The textual critic knows that, in most cases, the available manuscripts are descended from a single original. If the manuscripts of Mark's gospel do not agree in recording a particular saying, only one version can be correct. Mark wrote X, or Y, or Z. If he wrote X, then Y and Z are corruptions. Similarly, if Jesus had one standard form for every parable and every saying, every variation from this standard form must be a later corruption.

In Joseph Baird's opinion, those who argue in this way display an ignorance of what is involved in the life of a travelling preacher, which Baird regards as possibly a side effect of academic isolation.[16] Dorothy Sayers went further. Sayers saw the "law of non-repetition" as a symptom of christological heresy, a twentieth-century form of the ancient heresy of docetism. Those who alleged that Jesus never repeated himself, or that if he did it was always in identical words, were not in her opinion thinking of Jesus as a real human being.[17]

John D. Crossan has examined the belief of Dorothy Sayers and others that Jesus repeated his stories with variations. He quotes the statement of Robert W. Funk that it would be more accurate to speak of independent traditions than of one original parable, and comments that

> In most cases, however, when one compares independent versions of a parable, one is usually constrained to take one over another as "more original," that is, closer to that which is taken as coming from the historical Jesus. One seldom ends up with two or more equally good variations.[18]

There are at least two assumptions behind this argument. The first assumption is that there are criteria by which we can assess which gospel parables are "good" and which are less good. For example, the presence or absence of allegory in a parable has often been used as a criterion of its badness or goodness. The second assumption is that, having determined which is the "good" version, only that version can be credited to Jesus. Features such as allegory may be acceptable in a

---

[16]Joseph Arthur Baird, *Audience Criticism and the Historical Jesus* (Philadelphia: Westminster Press, 1969) 166-67.

[17]Dorothy Leigh Sayers, *Unpopular Opinions* (London: Victor Gollancz, 1946) 27.

[18]Crossan, *In Parables,* 117-18.

first-century rabbi, or in an early Christian, but Jesus can only have spoken parables in their pure form. Both these assumptions seem to me to be much more questionable than is commonly recognized.

Poets Are Not Logical

A great deal of the New Testament is poetic in structure. Many sayings of Jesus follow the rhythmic patterns of Hebrew poetry. In the more poetic sections of Paul's letters, such as Philippians 2:5-11, many scholars believe Paul was quoting early Christian hymns. And there certainly are hymns in the New Testament— the songs of Mary, Zechariah, and Simeon in Luke's gospel, and the songs of heaven in the Revelation of John. The boundary between poetry and prose is not always easy to draw, and much of the New Testament lies on the boundary line.

Isma'il R. al-Faruqi has suggested that the poetic element in the Bible is a particular problem for scholars in the Western world:

> Like the ancient Hellenes', the Western mind does not seem to have the capacity to take Semitic anthropomorphisms, figures of speech, allegories, and the like, poetically. The Semitic notion of transcendence was lost to the Christian tradition because transcendent truth can be expressed only in poetical language.[19]

Dorothy Sayers believed that, whereas the error of the Middle Ages was to use poetic techniques to investigate scientific questions, since the seventeenth century we have tended to the opposite error. We use the quantitative methods of science to investigate poetic truth. The Royal Society announced in 1687 that they "exacted from their members a close, naked, *natural* way of speaking . . . bringing all things as near the mathematical plainness as they can." Such a style may indeed be appropriate to a technical journal; but Sayers protested that, to the poet, the mathematical way of speaking is not "natural" at all. The words of a poet must never be interpreted absolutely, but only in relation to their context. They must be considered as fields of force, which disturb or are disturbed by their environment.[20]

One man who tried to apply logic to poetry was the great textual critic Richard Bentley. In A. E. Housman's opinion Bentley, born in 1662, shared the prosaic mind of his age and, for all his learning, was never able to appreciate poetry. We can see the results of this in his edition of *Paradise Lost*.[21]

---

[19]Isma'il R. al-Faruqi, *International Review of Missions* 65 (October 1976): 386.

[20]Sayers, *Unpopular Opinions,* 48-56.

[21]Alfred Edward Housman, *Selected Prose* (Cambridge: Cambridge University Press, 1961) 12.

Bentley believed that, after Milton became blind, an unscrupulous person corrupted his original script. The text reads that "four speedy Cherubim" were sent out with trumpets to summon an assembly. In Bentley's view "speedy" was a corruption of "sturdy," since what was needed to blow a good blast was not speed but strength. Similarly, the text describes how Uriel brought a message to Paradise at sunset: "Thither came Uriel, gliding through the even." Bentley altered "even" to "heaven," on the grounds that evening is a division of time, not of space, and you can no more glide through the even that you can glide through six o'clock.[22]

Housman could see a pattern in emendations such as these. Bentley, he believed, like many scholars with prosaic minds, was trying to make the author conform to a logical pattern of his own invention.

> His buoyant mind, elated by the exercise of its powers, often forgot the nature of its business, and turned from work to play; and many a time when he feigned and half fancied that he was correcting the scribe, he knew in his heart (and of his *Paradise Lost* they tell us he confessed it) that he was revising the author.[23]

The habit of revising the author has a long pedigree. For some 150 years Shakespeare's play *King Lear* was acted in England not as Shakespeare wrote it, but in the revised version of Nahum Tate. Alfred Harbage has described the principles on which Tate based his revision. He regarded the original play as "a heap of Jewels, unstrung and unpolisht." What was lacking was "regularity and probability," which Tate provided by granting success to the "innocent distrest persons." Edgar married Cordelia, and everyone was rescued but the villains. Charles Gildon in 1710 defended this procedure, and invoked Aristotle's statement that Tragedy "by means of Terror and Compassion perfectly refines in us all sorts of Passions." In *King Lear,* Gildon continued,

> the King and Cordelia ought by no means to have died, and therefore Mr. Tate has very justly alter'd that Particular, which must disgust the Reader and Audience, to have Vertue and Piety meet so unjust a Reward. So that this plot, tho of so celebrated a Play, has none of the ends of Tragedy, moving neither Fear nor Pity.[24]

We may call this the logical approach to literature. It assumes that authors should conform to a set pattern laid down by the critic, and revises them if they do not.

---

[22]Ibid., 13.

[23]Ibid., 29.

[24]Alfred Harbage, *Conceptions of Shakespeare* (Cambridge MA: Harvard University Press, 1966) 81.

The parables of Jesus have been prime victims of the logical approach to literature. Critics have regarded them, not as works of art, but as set pieces, which have to conform to fixed rules. Two rules that gained wide acceptance in the first half of the twentieth century, but in recent years have come under increasing attack, are (1) the rule that there can be no allegory in a genuine parable and (2) the rule that a genuine parable has only one point. Let us look at these rules in more detail.

(1) *Parable and allegory.* In his pioneering book *The Parables of Jesus,* first published a century ago, Adolf Jülicher drew a clear distinction between parable and allegory. The parable is a true-to-life story, the details of which are only important because they make the story as a whole more lifelike. In the allegory, on the other hand, every detail has a hidden, symbolic meaning, and only those who have the key can understand the meaning.[25]

According to Jülicher, these two types of story could not be combined: "Half allegory and half fable are only mythological entities." Jesus must have consistently used either the one or the other. In Jülicher's opinion Jesus only spoke "parables." Wherever stories are recorded in the gospels with allegorical details, these details do not go back to Jesus but are later additions. It is the task of the modern critic to recover the original parable by stripping away these additions.

Jülicher has had many disciples in the twentieth century. Norman Perrin, for example, describes parable and allegory as two incompatible approaches to communication—the one pictorial and direct, the other symbolic and hidden.[26] Other critics, however, have rejected this either/or distinction. In his study of the rabbinic parables Paul Fiebig pointed out that many of them contained allegorical elements, and concluded, "I would characterize the Jewish similitudes as parables with a mixture of allegory." Robert H. Stein agrees with Fiebig, and asserts that Jülicher depended on Aristotle and Greek theories of rhetoric in depicting the nature of a parable, rather than on the Old Testament.[27]

The Hebrew term מָשָׁל (*mashal*) covered a wide range of story, from proverbial sayings (1 Samuel 10:12; Proverbs 10:1) to elaborate allegories (Ezekiel 17:2; 24:3). Similarly the Greek word παραβολή (*parabolē*) ranged in meaning from proverbial sayings such as "physician, heal thyself" (Luke 4:23) to the symbolic

---

[25]Adolf Jülicher, *The Parables of Jesus,* as translated and quoted in Werner George Kümmel, *The New Testament: The History of the Investigation of Its Problems,* trans. S. McLean Gilmour and Howard C. Kee (London: SCM Press; Nashville/New York: Abingdon Press, 1972) 186-88.

[26]Norman Perrin, *Rediscovering the Teaching of Jesus* (London: SCM Press, 1967) 257.

[27]Robert H. Stein, *An Introduction to the Parables of Jesus* (Philadelphia: Westminster Press, 1981) 54, quoting Paul Fiebig, *Altjüdische Gleichnisse und die Geschichte Jesu* (Tübingen: J. C. B. Mohr, 1904).

significance of the Old Testament tabernacle (Hebrews 9:9). Parable and allegory are not opposites. They are like adjacent colors in a rainbow which merge into each other at their points of contact.

We should therefore not try to squeeze the parables of Jesus into a predetermined mold, but look at each parable independently. On the one hand, we should not give a hidden meaning to every detail of every parable. We should not interpret the parable of the Good Samaritan in Augustine's way (the thieves are the devil and his angels, the inn is the church, and so on),[28] or in an equivalent modern way (the thieves are modern critics and the donkey is the Westminster Confession). This is not what Jesus meant, and Jülicher's approach was a healthy reaction against that kind of allegorizing. But on the other hand, where the gospel writers report that Jesus used allegory, we should not rule this out on dogmatic grounds. Why should Jesus—who was familiar, for example, with the Old Testament in all its variety—have limited himself to only one of the story forms he found appropriate?

(2) *One point only.* The second rule is that a genuine parable is designed to make one single point. A good example of this rule in operation is C. H. Dodd's comment on the parable of the Seed Growing Secretly.

> The application of the parable is simple and direct: the Kingdom of God is like this. It is true that we are still uncertain whether the Kingdom of God is like the seed, or like what happens when the seed is sown: whether it is like the growth or like the harvest. There is therefore a difficult problem of interpretation.[29]

The problem was of Dodd's own making. By insisting that a parable could have only one point, he was unable to treat a story as a story. He defined a parable as "normally the dramatic presentation of a situation, intended to suggest vividly some single idea."[30] But how can any dramatic presentation be limited in this way? Does it make sense to ask what is the one single idea conveyed by Shakespeare's *King Lear*?

Dan O. Via objects to this way of treating the parables. A parable, he insists, is a story, and the teller of the story is interested, not only in making a theological point, but also in the story itself. There is more than one important element in a parable, and the structure of connections of these elements is not determined by events or ideas outside the parable but by the author's creative composition. By

---

[28]For a more detailed critique of Augustine's interpretation, see Dodd, *Parables,* 13-14 (USA 1-2).

[29]Ibid., 132 (USA 141).

[30]Ibid., 123 (USA 131).

contrast, the one-point approach sees the meaning of a parable in one isolated factor that is connected with a situation outside the parable. In Via's opinion this approach is only less allegorizing in degree than the old precritical allegorizing, since it breaks the internal coherence of the story.[31]

Sallie McFague TeSelle is equally insistent that a parable should be valued as a story in its own right, not just as an illustration of a point. She describes parables as "extended metaphors," and insists that a metaphor cannot be reduced to one point, nor can its meaning be "foreclosed in some historical moment." We should not say that the parable "has a point" or teaches a lesson, but that it is itself what it is talking about. The parable of the Prodigal Son has meaning beyond the story of a human father and his wayward son, and tells us about the love of God; but it does so indirectly, as the story itself absorbs our interest. "We do not, I think, naturally allegorize it. (Is the father 'God'? Is the feast a symbol of 'the Kingdom'?) The story is 'thick' not transparent; like a painting, it is looked *at,* not through."[32]

Authors and Preachers Adapt Their Style to Their Audience

There is a well-known story about Charles Dodgson, the Oxford mathematics don who wrote *Alice in Wonderland* under the pseudonym of Lewis Carroll. According to the story, Queen Victoria enjoyed *Alice* so much that she asked for the author's other books, and was given some of his mathematical works. The story is untrue, and Dodgson officially denied it. Nevertheless, it is interesting to speculate what Queen Victoria would have made of the contrast between Dodgson the mathematician and Carroll the storyteller. A literary critic could, no doubt, detect some similarities between the two; but in books on such different subjects intended for such different readers the differences are likely to be far more striking than the similarities.[33]

The thirteen letters bearing Paul's name were addressed to a similar variety of individuals and groups. Compare, for example, the letters to the Corinthians with the letters to Timothy and Titus. Most of the Corinthian Christians were poorly educated and economically deprived.[34] Some would be slaves, some would be illiterate. When he preached to them, he "did not use big words and great learning"

---

[31]Dan Otto Via, *The Parables* (Philadelphia: Fortress Press, 1967) 25, 89.

[32]Sallie McFague TeSelle, *Speaking in Parables* (Philadelphia: Fortress Press, 1975) 5.

[33]Jean Gattégno, *Lewis Carroll: Fragments of a Looking-glass,* trans. Rosemary Sheed (New York: Crowell, 1976; London: Allen & Unwin, 1977) 288.

[34]1 Corinthians 1:26-31.

(1 Corinthians 2:1),[35] and the same would be true when he wrote them a letter. Timothy and Titus, on the other hand, had probably had a good education. It therefore comes as no surprise to find a very limited vocabulary in the Corinthian letters, and a much wider and more educated vocabulary in the letters to Timothy and Titus. What is surprising is the assumption that is sometimes made that this difference in vocabulary indicates, not a difference in readership, but a difference in authorship.

The Corinthian church was a difficult church. Paul had to go back to basic principles, and explain things as far as possible in "words of one syllable." He thought of them as still children (1 Corinthians 3:1-3). It is rare for anyone to address children and adults in the same style. In the introduction to her book of nursery school sketches, Joyce Grenfell noted how most of us put on a special voice when speaking to infants that we would not use in talking to people of our own age.

> My father was the only person I ever knew who addressed babies in prams as if they were his contemporaries. He spoke as he would to a bank manager or a bishop, friendly but respectful. Sometimes a tiny eyebrow may have been raised, but a look of interest took over and the pleasing pink blob of a small face registered relief and rapport.[36]

I am not suggesting that Paul wrote to the Corinthians in baby language. What I am suggesting is that Paul, unlike Joyce Grenfell's father, addressed different people in different ways. In writing to his colleagues Timothy and Titus he felt free to use words and ideas he was unwilling to use in writing to the Corinthians. As J. A. T. Robinson has observed, Paul would not be the last church leader whose style and subject matter in a letter to his ordained colleagues differed markedly from his manner of speaking and writing to wider audiences.[37]

In adapting his language to his readers, Paul was following good twentieth-century principles. In the field of modern Bible translation the style of a particular translation will depend on the public for which it is intended. The Good News Bible is a "common language translation," intended for people of an average level of education. The New English Bible and the Revised English Bible are more literary translations, and will probably be enjoyed most by those who have had a college education or equivalent. The contrast between the vocabularies of these translations is similar to the contrast between the vocabularies of 1 and 2 Corinthians on the one hand, and the letters to Timothy and Titus on the other.

---

[35]Good News Bible, a.k.a. Today's English Version.

[36]Joyce Grenfell, *George—Don't Do That . . .* (London: Futura Publications Ltd., 1978) 13-15.

[37]John Arthur Thomas Robinson, *Redating the New Testament* (London: SCM Press, 1976) 70.

Luke was another author who could vary his style to suit his readers. The preface to Luke's gospel is written in the formal style in which prefaces were normally written at that time. The rest of the gospel is written in a more simple, popular style. This variation is natural in the circumstances. In the preface Luke was addressing Theophilus, who was probably an educated man who would appreciate good Greek. In the gospel as a whole Luke was hoping to reach a much wider circle, and therefore adopted a "common language" style of presentation.

In his book *Communicating Conviction* Peter Brooks makes the point that, if communication is to take place, the words of the speaker or writer must match the experience of the hearer or reader. He illustrates this from Charles Kraft's study of the communication methods of Jesus. Kraft states four principles, which could be described as a summary of the communication theory to which Jesus worked. The first of these principles is

> For information to be conveyed accurately both the giver and the receiver of the information must operate within the same frame of reference.

This, comments Brooks, was certainly true of the teaching of Jesus. Because of the incarnation, Jesus was able to share a common frame of reference with his hearers. The sower and the fisherman, the housewife and the neighbor, were not decorative additions to a teaching given in the form of propositions or concepts. It was through a shared experience of the behavior of well-known people that the message was communicated.[38]

The same could be said of the conversations Jesus had with Jerusalem rabbis. Because of the time he had spent in the synagogue and the temple, listening to the rabbis and asking them questions, Jesus was able to share their frame of reference just as much as he shared that of Galilean peasants. But to do so would of necessity involve a change of style and vocabulary. Those who declare that Jesus always spoke in one consistent style are in fact alleging that Jesus was a poor communicator.

The teaching of Jesus was largely in the form of dialogue—either explicit dialogue with individuals, disciples, and scribes, or what Brooks calls implicit dialogue with the unspoken thoughts of the hearers.[39] For this reason the audiences Jesus addressed form an important part of the gospel record. Joseph Baird has examined the 422 separate units in Huck-Lietzmann's *Synopsis of the First Three Gospels,* and reckons that in 395, or ninety-four percent, of them the audience is

---

[38]Peter Brooks, *Communicating Conviction* (London: Epworth Press, 1983) 98-101, quoting Charles Kraft, "The Incarnation, Cross-Cultural Communication and Communication Theory," *Evangelical Missions Quarterly* (Summer 1973).

[39]Brooks, *Communicating Conviction,* 86.

clearly designated. He draws from this fact the natural conclusion. The gospel writers, and the sources they used, believed the teaching of Jesus was audience centered. The gospels were not anthologies of theological texts and moral stories; they were living dramas.[40]

When Shakespeare records the speeches of Brutus and Mark Antony after the death of Julius Caesar, the reactions of the audience form an integral part of their speeches. They were not giving lectures on the tragedy of death, but living speeches to a living audience. The speeches and sayings of Jesus were alive in the same way. They were not floating fragments of tradition, preserved in a kind of featureless limbo by the early church, and resurrected in an artificial context by the gospel writers. They formed part of dramatic stories, in which what Jesus said and did, and what his audience said and did, were from the beginning indivisible parts of a single whole.

When Dorothy Sayers was writing her radio plays about the ministry of Jesus, she found that the dramatic reality of the life and teaching of Jesus appeared more vividly in John's gospel than in any of the others. It was John who recorded, not only what Jesus said, but what the other people said to him, who reproduced the cut-and-thrust of controversy and the development of an argument. When John was the authority for any scene, Sayers found her task as playwright to be easy. Either the dialogue was all there—vivid and personal on both sides—or the part of the partner in dialogue could be readily reconstructed from the replies given.[41]

This raises the question whether the dramatic dialogues in John's gospel were a literary device of the author or were based on recollections of eyewitnesses. There is a sharp contrast in style between the teaching of Jesus recorded in John's gospel (mainly conversation with Jewish theologians or private conversation with his disciples) and the teaching recorded in the other three gospels (mainly open-air preaching to crowds in Galilee). Many scholars have assumed that Jesus could not have spoken in two different styles. David Friedrich Strauss pioneered what Werner Georg Kümmel calls the "consistently historical" approach to the New Testament. This approach requires Jesus also to be consistent: either he spoke in the style recorded in the Synoptic Gospels or he spoke in the style recorded by John.[42] In Dorothy Sayers's opinion, however, it was natural for Jesus to adapt his style to his audience. Had Jesus been someone who had died within living memory, and

---

[40]Baird, *Audience Criticism*, 32, 134. Baird cites Albert Huck and Hans Lietzmann, *Synopsis of the First Three Gospels*, 9th ed. rev., trans. and ed. by F. L. Cross (New York: American Bible Society, 1936ff.; Oxford: Basil Blackwell, 1951ff.).

[41]Sayers, *Man Born to be King*, 33-34.

[42]Strauss's *Life of Jesus* as translated and quoted in Kümmel, *The New Testament*, 125. "The Consistently Historical Approach to the New Testament" is Kümmel's title for part 4 (pp. 120-205) of *The New Testament*, in which he cites and discusses Strauss and others.

John a modern author, Sayers imagined a newspaper review of the *Memoirs of Jesus Christ by John Bar-Zebedee* might run like this:

> The most interesting and important portions of the book are those devoted to Christ's lectures in the Temple and the theological and philosophical instructions given privately to His followers. These, naturally, differ considerably in matter and manner from the open-air "talks" delivered before a mixed audience, and shed a flood of new light, both on the massive intellectual equipment of the preacher, and on the truly astonishing nature of His claim to authority.[43]

Authors and Preachers Adapt Their Language to Their Situation

According to Mark's gospel, Jesus was inconsistent. Sometimes he told the people he healed to keep quiet about what had happened; at other times he told them to tell others. There are two ways of explaining this inconsistency—the situational and the logical.

The situational approach regards Jesus as a pastoral counsellor as well as a physical healer. It is essential for a pastoral counsellor to be flexible, and not to have a cut-and-dried answer to every situation. Since the circumstances of each healing varied, the advice Jesus gave to the people healed would also vary.

The logical approach was pioneered by William Wrede in his book *The Messianic Secret in the Gospels*. Wrede believed that "it is the explanation which exhibits a unity of conception that is most conclusive," and that "all those explanations at once fall to the ground which can only illuminate individual passages. For they presuppose a plurality or an alteration of motivations for the prohibitions Jesus utters." Since he could not find a motivation which could apply equally to all the passages, Wrede concluded that there was "an inner contradiction in Mark's presentation." This was because Mark was a "painfully naive author of antiquity," who "did not think through from one point in his presentation to the next." The whole concept of a Messianic Secret was, in Wrede's opinion, too inconsistent to be historical; it was an example of Mark's attempt "somewhat gauchely . . . to fashion history out of ideas."[44]

Wrede's approach was not at first taken seriously in the English-speaking world. William Sanday compared Wrede's style to that of a Prussian official: "His mind is mathematical, with something of the stiffness of mathematics—a mind of the type which is supposed to ask of everything, What does it prove? It is a mind

---

[43]Sayers, *Unpopular Opinions*, 26.

[44]Wrede, *Secret*, 37-39, 17, 132, 135.

that applies the standards to which it is accustomed with very little play of historical imagination.''[45] Sanday rightly felt that historical imagination was of more importance in literary criticism than mathematical logic. The situational approach may leave too much to the imagination, and because of our ignorance of the historical background may force us to leave many questions unanswered, but it does at least have the advantage of regarding Jesus as a genuine human being, who could adapt to circumstances rather than following a predetermined formula.

The same principle applies to the New Testament epistles. The contents of any letter are determined by the circumstances under which the letter is written. This may seem obvious, but it is often forgotten. A writer such as Paul is expected to say X or Y, not because X or Y would be the appropriate message in a particular situation, but because Paul, being Paul, would be bound to say X or Y whenever he put pen to paper. Only those letters that major in justification by faith can be genuinely Pauline.

The logical approach lays great stress on vocabulary. Certain words are regarded as ''characteristic'' of an author. If the author deals with a new subject and uses new words, these words are uncharacteristic, and bring that person's authorship into question. The problem with this approach is that any book by any author is likely to contain a large number of unusual words. Humphrey Palmer spells this out:

> In a story of [Aleksandr Sergeyevich] Pushkin's totalling 29,345 words, 4,783 *different* words were used, 2,384 of them only once (just over half). . . . This ''tail'' of rare words in a frequency distribution is longer in some authors than others, but is long in all texts, even a Basic English version of St. John.[44]

A good example of the problem of uncharacteristic words is the parable of the Sower and its interpretation. C. H. Dodd believed Jesus spoke the parable, but that the interpretation was added by the early church. One of his reasons for believing this was the interpretation's vocabulary. He noted that the whole passage was strikingly unlike the majority of the sayings of Jesus, and included within a few verses seven words that were not proper to the rest of the synoptic record. All seven were characteristic of the vocabulary of Paul, and most of them occurred also in other apostolic writers. ''These facts,'' Dodd concluded, ''create at once

---

[45]William Sanday, *The Life of Christ in Recent Research* (Oxford: Oxford University Press, 1907) 70-71.

[46]Humphrey Palmer, *The Logic of Gospel Criticism* (London: Macmillan; New York: St. Martin's Press, 1968) 221. Palmer's source for counts of Pushkin's *Captain's Daughter* is B. Epstein in *The Russian Word Count*, ed. H. H. Josselson (1953) 25-26. His information regarding the Basic English version of John is taken from George Udny Yule, *The Statistical Study of Literary Vocabulary* (Cambridge: Cambridge University Press, 1944) 22.

a presumption that we have here not a part of the primitive tradition of the words of Jesus, but a piece of apostolic teaching.''[47]

Scholars discussing whether or not Paul wrote the Pastoral Epistles use the same method as Dodd. They compile lists of words which occur in these letters, but not in Paul's letters to churches, and use these lists to ''create a presumption'' about authorship. But statistics about rare words are of limited value. Humphrey Palmer comments that ''there are, indeed, several unusual words in Mark's explanation of the parables . . . but then every writer's vocabulary consists largely of unusual words.''[48] It may be better to follow the principle laid down by George Yule in his *Statistical Study of Literary Vocabulary* that ''the savor of an author's text must . . . be determined in the main not by the exceptional words but by the common words.''[49]

Here also, however, we need to be cautious. Paul, as a travelling preacher, was continually facing new situations. These situations influenced, not only the vocabulary, but also the general style of his letters. The letters written in the heat of controversy have a controversial style, with short sentences and rhetorical questions. The letter to the Ephesians has long sentences and no rhetorical questions. This contrast seemed natural to William Barclay, given the circumstances. At the end of his life Paul was in prison, and had time to meditate that he had not had earlier in his ministry. Is it any wonder, Barclay asks, that the style of Ephesians is not the style of the earlier letters?[50]

The tailor who makes clothes to measure can never match the consistency of clothes mass-produced in a factory. Paul's letters were made-to-measure. The spiritual measurements of the various churches determined the shape and style of each letter. Failure to recognize this is a serious weakness in the statistical approach to questions of authorship. A. Q. Morton has counted, in each of Paul's letters, the number of times per sentence that καί (*kai*) and δέ (*de*), Greek words for ''and,'' occur.[51] What should we deduce from these statistics? The frequency of the word ''and'' largely depends on the length of sentences, and the length of sentences depends on the style of the letter, and the style of the letter depends on the circumstances under which it was written. In George Caird's words,

> The sentence ''God forbid'' occurs ten times in Romans, and it is hardly surprising that the incidence of *kai* for these ten sentences is below average. . . .

---

[47]Dodd, *Parables,* 14-15.

[48]Palmer, *Gospel Criticism,* 157.

[49]Yule, *Statistical Study,* 222.

[50]William Barclay, *The Letters to the Galatians and Ephesians,* Daily Study Bible (Edinburgh: The Saint Andrew Press; Philadelphia: Westminster Press, 1958) 75-76.

[51]Morton and McLeman, *Christianity and the Computer.*

In fact, the short sentence and asyndeton are typical of Paul's debating style, and we may not use this style as a criterion of authorship unless we suppose him incapable of opening his mouth without arguing.[52]

Authors and Preachers Develop with Time

One of P. G. Wodehouse's characters, J. Hamilton Beamish, was author of the famous Beamish booklets on business acumen and driving power. In his booklet *The Marriage Sane* he argued that "the mating of the sexes should be a reasoned process, ruled by the intellect." It was therefore a surprise to his friend Molly when he told her that he had fallen in love with a girl on the bus and did not know her name.

"You have fallen in love with a girl and you don't know who she is? I thought you always said that love was a reasoned emotion and all that."
"One's views alter," said Hamilton Beamish. "A man's intellectual perceptions do not stand still. One develops."[53]

The capacity of an author to develop is not peculiar to Hamilton Beamish. The letters of Paul show evidence of development. For example, his expectation that Christ would return to earth in his lifetime grew less as he grew older. But how far did the development in Paul's thinking affect his style of writing? The letters to Timothy and Titus bear Paul's name, and refer to his being at the end of his life. Their style is different in various respects from that of Paul's letters to churches. How far should old age and changed circumstances be taken into account in estimating what Paul was capable of writing? This question cannot be answered by feeding lists of words into a computer. It is not a question of determining more exactly where the differences lie (which a computer can do) but of relating those differences to the character of a human being whose intellectual perceptions did not stand still and who was continually developing.

The interval between Paul's first and last letters may be compared to the interval between the first and last plays of Shakespeare. The change in Shakespeare's style is remarkable. As G. B. Harrison observed, if we compare *The Tempest* with Shakespeare's other fairy play *A Midsummer Night's Dream*, and set any speeches of the two plays alongside one another, it will be clear how far Shakespeare travelled in less than twenty years.[54]

---

[52]George Bradford Caird, "Do Computers Count," *Expository Times* 76 (1964/1965): 176. [*Sic*. There is no "?" in the ET title of the article.]

[53]Pelham Grenville Wodehouse, *The Small Bachelor* (London: Methuen, 1933) 68.

[54]George Bagshawe Harrison, introduction to *The Tempest* in *The Works of William Shakespeare*, vol. 2 (London: William Clowes & Sons Ltd., 1934) 327.

But it is not always necessary to wait twenty years to see an author's style change. Some readers of J. B. Priestley's novel *Faraway* found it disappointing. They felt that, after a good start in the first three chapters, the book then lost vitality. In his introduction Priestley explained the reason for this. There was an interval of several months between the writing of the first three chapters in England and the writing of the rest of the book after his research in the South Pacific. Following this hiatus he was like a car starting with a cold engine. He had lost his original momentum, and was carrying the extra burden of all the travel material, and admitted that, as a result, there was a loss of vitality in his writing.[55]

The few months that separated the two parts of Priestley's book resulted in a difference of style which several readers detected independently. In spite of this, readers of the book today accept it as a single work of art created by a single author. Unless they are literary archaeologists, they do not bother to speculate about the stages in its composition; and unless they are New Testament scholars, they do not assume that differences in style indicate difference in authorship.

Inconsistency in an author is a sign that the author is a growing and developing person, not a machine. There is, however, one type of literature that does not develop. In his anthology of railroad detective stories Bryan Morgan included two stories by Freeman Wills Crofts. The two stories were separated by a time-gap of nearly thirty years—from 1921 to 1950. Morgan notes that one could barely detect this time-gap from the style of the two stories, and attributes this to the fact that Crofts was a professional engineer as well as a professional author. "He wrote in a kind of dateless 'engineers' prose,' and paid comparatively little attention to character or the social scene."[55]

Authors who write in "engineers' prose," such as contributors to technical journals, may develop new vocabulary to keep pace with new discoveries, but their style of writing will remain fairly constant. They are not, like Shakespeare or Paul, appealing to the imagination as well as to the intellect of their readers, and striving to find new ways to express the inexpressible.

This raises the question whether academic scholars are the best equipped people to assess what Paul could or could not have written. For if there is an "engineers' prose," there is also an "academics' prose." Expertise in writing "academics' prose" may be more of a hindrance than a help when it comes to assessing, for example, whether Paul was capable of writing Ephesians.

---

[55]John Boynton Priestley, introduction to his *Faraway* (London: Pan Books Ltd., 1967) 5-6.

[56]Bryan Morgan, ed., *Crime on the Lines* (London: Routledge & Kegan Paul, 1975) xii.

Conclusion

"A foolish consistency," Emerson declared, "is the hobgoblin of little minds, adored by little statesmen and philosophers and divines. With consistency a great soul has simply nothing to do."[57] John Newman agreed: "Here below to live is to change, and to be perfect is to have changed often."[58] If this is true, the search for consistency in, say, the letters of Paul, is doomed to disappointment. There are indeed some fundamental convictions that underlie all that Paul wrote. But in point of detail each letter is unique, and reflects the reaction of a changing man to a new situation. Humphrey Palmer's summing up is sound:

> To distinguish two works as of different authorship we must (a) point out differences in style, and then (b) judge that one man *could not have* written in two styles so different. . . . New Testament writings are too short and specialized for judgments of style, with or without numbers, to carry much weight in decisions about authorship.[59]

---

[57]Ralph Waldo Emerson, "Self-Reliance," in *Essays,* first series (1841) #14.

[58]John Henry Newman, *Apologia pro Vita Sua* (1864).

[59]Palmer, *Gospel Criticism,* 224.

The Argument from Specialization

7

A scholar, unless by accident, is not a literary critic.   —A. E. Housman[1]

We live today in a world of specialists. To find out tomorrow's weather, we do not simply rely on the state of grandfather's rheumatism; we listen to the weather expert on radio or television. There are specialists to tell us what food we should eat, how we should invest our money, how we should do almost everything. We listen to their advice with respect, but we do not always follow it. Experience tells us that, on occasion, grandfather's rheumatism may be a better guide to our local weather than the forecast of the experts.

In this chapter I shall consider the role of specialization in New Testament study. I wish to indicate some of the problems involved in specialization, and also suggest some areas of expertise in which the nonspecialist may have the advantage.

The Problems of Specialization

(1) *The problem of limited uniqueness.* "Experto credité," said Virgil—trust the expert, the person with experience.[2] But who is the expert when it comes to study of the New Testament? One possible answer to that question is suggested by John Bowden:

Scholars working in other areas, lawyers, historians, literary critics, and systematic theologians, may tend to underestimate New Testament scholarship. They may not only share their experience with the New Testament critic when he asks for it, but also go on to tell him how to do his own work as well.[3]

---

[1]Alfred Edward Housman, *The Confines of Criticism* (Cambridge: Cambridge University Press, 1969) 26.

[2]Virgil, *Aeneid* 11.283.

[3]John Bowden, "Great Expectations? The New Testament Critic and His Audience," in *What about the New Testament?*, ed. M. D. Hooker and Colin J. A. Hickling (London: SCM Press, 1975) 2.

In this statement Bowden draws a distinction between "New Testament critics" on the one hand and "scholars working in other areas" on the other hand. He implies that the latter group should only express an opinion about the New Testament if their opinion is asked for. His reason, I presume, is that he regards study of the New Testament as a specialist field of study, in which New Testament critics are experts, but scholars working in other areas are amateurs.

But is this in fact the case? Is the history of the early church a unique branch of history, to be studied in isolation, or is it part of the history of the ancient world as a whole? Is the literature of the New Testament a unique form of literature, to be criticized by unique methods, or is it part of Greek literature, and of the history of literature through the ages?

In his famous contribution to the symposium *Essays and Reviews* in 1860, Benjamin Jowett stated that, in most respects, the New Testament should be treated as any other book. It is subject to the same rules of grammar and interpretation as any other Greek literature. Jowett's essay was welcomed in its day as a break-through—the emancipation of New Testament study from the clutches of the theologians—and its standpoint is still influential. But there have always been contrary voices.[4]

In his inaugural lecture *Queen or Cinderella?* C. F. Evans quoted the words of Albert Schweitzer:

> . . . the problem of the life of Jesus has no analogue in the field of history. . . . The standards of ordinary historical science are here inadequate, its methods not immediately applicable. The historical study of the life of Jesus has had to create its own methods for itself.[5]

This, commented Evans, was "something of an exaggeration." Critical investigation of the Bible in the nineteenth century grew up alongside the application of similar methods to secular literature. Nevertheless, Schweitzer's belief that scholars analyzing the gospels should make up their own rules has been widely accepted.

In Anthony Hanson's opinion this is particularly true of the form critics. Hanson describes form critics as "a peculiar group who have evolved criteria of evidence all their own." They use these criteria to decide whether stories in the gospels are authentic or not; but if the same criteria were applied to "secular" history, they could be used to discredit the accuracy of almost any historical document.[6]

---

[4]Benjamin Jowett, "On the Interpretation of Scripture," in *Essays and Reviews,* ed. J. Parker (London: Longman, 1860) 407-409.

[5]Christopher F. Evans, *Queen or Cinderella?* (Durham: University of Durham, 1960) 6. Evans quotes Albert Schweitzer, *The Quest of the Historical Jesus,* trans. W. Montgomery (London: A & C Black, 1910; New York: Macmillan, 1961) 6.

[6]Anthony Tyrrell Hanson, "The Quandary of Historical Scepticism," in *Vindications,* ed. A. T. Hanson (London: SCM Press, 1966) 94.

To illustrate his point Hanson applies form-critical methods to an extract from the ancient Jewish historian Josephus. The use of form-critical criteria casts doubt on almost everything in the passage. This is not, Hanson believes, because Josephus was a particularly unreliable writer, but because the same method will produce the same results, whichever writer it is applied to.[7]

Dennis E. Nineham disagrees with Hanson, not only because of his lower estimate of Josephus as a historian, but for a more fundamental reason:

> The nature of Josephus's writings and the character and history of his sources are so different from those of the gospels that it is in any case highly unlikely that any argument would lie from the one to the other.[8]

This statement agrees with that of Schweitzer: the gospels are regarded as a unique form of literature, which cannot be criticized by the same techniques as "secular" literature. As a result, the form-critical method becomes immune to criticism. We do not know the sources used by the gospel writers. The sources the form critics assume them to have used are the products of scholarly guesses rather than of weight of evidence. Yet if anyone tries to check the validity of the form-critical method by trying it out on other literature, he is told that the nature of these hypothetical sources makes any such comparison invalid. Jowett's insistence that the New Testament must be treated like any other book is denied at a stroke.

This argument is a retreat into obscurantism. If the gospels are unique in such a way that normal standards of criticism do not apply to them, ordinary Christians are forced to rely on the authority of those experts who alone know the correct techniques. Interpreting the gospels becomes the prerogative of a self-perpetuating oligarchy.

(2) *The problem of limited vision.* There is a sense in which every specialist has to be narrow-minded. As Magnus Pyke says, not only may a specialist in biology be incomprehensible to a chemist or a geologist; even within one discipline the divisions multiply:

> . . . paint chemists and dye chemists; men who study the chemistry of the aroma of port wine; those who investigate the chemical structure of plastic sheets or lubricating oil; less and less easily can they understand each other, even though they are all chemists.[9]

---

[7]Ibid., 83-89.

[8]Dennis E. Nineham, "Et hoc genus omne," in *Christian History and Interpretation: Studies Presented to John Knox,* ed. W. R. Farmer, C. F. D. Moule, and R. R. Niebuhr (Cambridge: Cambridge University Press, 1967)214.

[9]Magnus Pyke, *There and Back* (London: John Murray, 1978) 82.

Edward de Bono has pointed out one result of this tendency. With the mass of printed words doubling itself every ten years, scholars are no longer able to survey the whole field of scholarship and draw ideas from here and there. They only have time to study those ideas which are "relevant" to their specialties, and as a result are less likely to have their preconceived ideas radically changed. For, as de Bono says, "by definition relevance implies preconceived ideas."[10]

Marc Bloch has summed up well the pros and cons of specialization:

> Science dissects reality only in order to observe it better by virtue of a play of converging searchlights whose beams continually intermingle and interpenetrate each other. Danger threatens only when each searchlight operator claims to see everything by himself, when each canton of learning pretends to national sovereignty.[11]

To avoid this danger the specialist needs to be open to what is going on round about. The study of fragments, Bloch insists, will never produce knowledge of the whole, and will not even produce knowledge of the fragments. In order to understand one's own methods of investigation, one must see their connection with simultaneous tendencies in other fields.[12]

In Bloch's observation, the most successful craftsmen in one particular area of science were often "refugees from neighboring areas." For example, Pasteur, who renovated biology, was not a biologist, and during his lifetime was often made aware of this.[13] In similar vein, Helen Gardner noted how the study of English at Oxford University was pioneered by scholars trained in the Classics and in History. In her opinion this was an advantage, and had prevented English from being regarded as an esoteric subject which could only be taught by those who had devoted themselves to it from their youth up.[14]

The insights of "refugees from neighboring areas" are especially important in a field of study as wide as the New Testament. A New Testament specialist, were such a person to exist, would need to be expert in ancient Greek grammar, ancient history, archaeology, literary criticism, statistics, philosophy, the history of interpretation, and many other things as well. No one individual can be expert in all these areas. A well-researched thesis on Paul's use of the aorist subjunctive

---

[10]Edward de Bono, *The Use of Lateral Thinking* (London: Penguin Books, 1971) 102-103.

[11]Marc Bloch, *The Historian's Craft* (Manchester: Manchester University Press, 1954) 150.

[12]Ibid., 18.

[13]Ibid., 21 n. 1.

[14]Helen Gardner, *Literary Studies* (Oxford: Oxford University Press, 1967) 12.

does not make its author competent to decide whether Paul wrote Ephesians, let alone deciding whether Jesus rose from the dead. An expert in one area of New Testament study is an amateur in another.

This raises an important question for the study of the New Testament. Who is competent to decide, let us say, whether or not Luke was a reliable historian? Is it the scholar who has spent his or her life studying the New Testament, but has only a limited knowledge of other historians? Or is it the scholar who has spent his or her life studying ancient Greek historians, but has only a limited knowledge of the New Testament? Or do we need both?

Stephen Neill thought it would be an excellent thing if scholars who wished to approach the New Testament in the light of history could be required to win their spurs elsewhere in the wide fields of ancient history, and only advance to historical study of the life of Jesus and the early church after having proved competent in other less difficult areas.[15] This, no doubt, is an ideal. In practice, can we expect those whose primary interest is theological to undertake this kind of historical discipline, or to refrain from comment on historical issues if they have not done so? Martin Hengel laments the fact that "theologians today increasingly lack historical knowledge and an interest in history."[16] But, given the pressures of specialization, can we expect expert historical knowledge from any but the minority of New Testament scholars for whom historical study is their major interest?

A similar question arises in respect of literary criticism. In 1959 C. S. Lewis declared his belief that some leading New Testament scholars lacked literary judgment, and did not perceive the true quality of the texts they were discussing. The reason for this, he suggested, could be the very fact that they had spent their lives studying the New Testament, and had not acquired the standards of comparison which could only come from a wide and deep and genial experience of literature in general. If a scholar told him that something in a gospel was legend or romance, he wanted to know how many legends or romances that scholar had read, how well his palate was trained in detecting them by the flavor, not how many years he had spent on that gospel.[17]

Roland M. Frye made a similar comment in his essay "A Literary Perspective for the Criticism of the Gospels" published in 1971. As Frye had read certain kinds of New Testament criticism, the methods were so different from those generally accepted in his field of English literature that he felt he was observing "a

[15]Stephen Charles Neill, *The Interpretation of the New Testament 1861–1961* (London, New York, Toronto: Oxford University Press, 1964) 279.

[16]Martin Hengel, *Acts and the History of Earliest Christianity,* trans. John Bowden (London: SCM Press, 1979) viii.

[17]C. S. Lewis, *Christian Reflections* (London: Collins, 1981) 193.

radically nonliterary enterprise at work." When considered from a professionally literary point of view, eisegesis too often seemed to supplant exegesis, speculation overshadowed evidence, and twentieth-century preconceptions reduced the gospels to a pale reflection of our own convictions.[18]

The situation today is very different from that of 1959 or 1971, with a much greater recognition of the relevance of literary critical techniques to New Testament study. Discussion of these techniques is beyond the scope of this book, nor am I competent to attempt it. My concern is that the comments of people like C. S. Lewis and Roland M. Frye should not be forgotten, and their implications should be recognized. We should not only ask what new insights the literary perspective gives us today, but also ask how far the absence of that perspective in the past invalidated the methods, and therefore the conclusions, of the scholars concerned.

In his preface to *Candid Questions Concerning Gospel Form Criticism* by Erhardt Güttgemanns, W. G. Doty explains his choice of the word "candid" to translate the German word "offen." The original word carries overtones of "frank, sincere," and this, Doty feels, is true of the book:

> It honestly expresses exasperation with a methodological ostrich-ism that has ducked its head into the sand more frequently, ignored nonreligious scholarship more completely, and pooh-poohed criticism from other academic disciplines more effectively, than now seems credible, given recent developments that have opened biblical studies towards literary-critical and other methodologies.[19]

If Doty's judgment is correct, we need to be on our guard. For the ostrich does not only bury its head in the sand; it also lays eggs to perpetuate its species.

(3) *The problem of credulous skepticism.* One of the dangers facing the specialist scholar is the temptation to skepticism. Scholars grow in knowledge by asking questions; and the habit of questioning everything can easily lead to the habit of believing no one and nothing, which is just as untrue to the facts of life as the habit of believing everyone and everything.

---

[18]Roland Mushat Frye, "A Literary Perspective for the Criticism of the Gospels," in *Jesus and Man's Hope,* vol. 2, ed. Donald G. Miller and Dikran Y. Hadidian (Pittsburgh: Pittsburgh Theological Seminary 1971) 194-95. See also esp. Frye's "The Synoptic Problem and Analogies in Other Literature," in *The Relationships among the Gospels: An Interdisciplinary Dialogue,* ed. William O. Walker, Jr., 261-302 (San Antonio TX: Trinity University Press, 1978), in which (301-302) Frye related this poignant anecdote: "After my paper 'A Literary Perspective for the Criticism of the Gospels' was read at the Pittsburgh Festival on the Gospels in 1970, the African scholar E. Bolaji Idowu commented that most New Testament criticism could be summed up in the words of Mary Magdalene at the empty tomb: 'They have taken my Lord away, and I know not where they have laid him.' "

[19]William G. Doty, translator's introduction to Erhardt Güttgemanns, *Candid Questions Concerning Gospel Form Criticism,* (Pittsburgh: Pickwick Press, 1979) xiii.

According to Herbert G. Wood the prime duty of the historian is to distinguish the certain from the probable and the probable from the possible. The temptation of the orthodox apologist is to upgrade possibilities into probabilities and probabilities into certainties. The temptation of the radical skeptic is the opposite: to downgrade certainties into probabilities and probabilities into possibilities. In either way, Wood declared, "the true balanced historical judgment" is lost.[20]

This lack of "balanced historical judgment" may help explain a curious fact—that skepticism is often combined with credulity. Marc Bloch saw this clearly. "Skepticism on principle," he wrote, "is neither a more estimable nor a more productive intellectual attitude than the credulity with which it is frequently blended in the simpler minds."[21] To link skepticism with credulity is not as strange as may appear. In most cases skepticism is selective. The point is well made by G. K. Clark:

> A man must believe something, and the fact that he has summarily rejected a great many things which other people believe is no guarantee that he is able to criticize whatever it is that he himself accepts.[22]

Clark goes on to comment on the "strange phenomenon" that some of the most unlikely beliefs that civilized people have ever entertained have been products of skepticism. He points out that any human transaction, if examined minutely, is likely to disclose some improbable elements, owing to the carelessness or eccentricity of the people concerned, or simply to coincidence. In normal circumstances these would not be worth noticing; but if the circumstances are momentous, they are put under the microscope and take on enormous proportions and a sinister meaning. As a result, instead of the simple explanation of the transaction, a more extravagant theory is accepted which, however improbable, covers the facts.

Clark quotes as an example a book on the murder of Abraham Lincoln, which finds the incompetence of the guards and the investigators so incredible that an elaborate theory is constructed of a conspiracy with Lincoln's colleagues. The events surrounding the death of President Kennedy produced similar results. In both these cases the momentous result of the event seems to have led to an exaggeration of the unlikelihood of the admitted improbabilities in the story, even

---

[20]Herbert George Wood, *Jesus in the Twentieth Century* (London: Lutterworth Press, 1960) 40.

[21]Bloch, *Historian's Craft*, 79-80.

[22]George Sidney Roberts Kitson Clark, *The Critical Historian* (London: Heinemann; New York: Basic Books, 1967) 8.

though, as Clark says, there is no logical reason why an aberration should be more improbable because its consequences are important.[23]

This mixture of skepticism and credulity is an important factor in modern criticism of the New Testament. A good example is the principle enunciated by Julius Wellhausen which, according to Rudolf Bultmann, should govern all research:

> We must recognize that a literary work or fragment of tradition is a primary source for the historical situation out of which it arose, and is only a secondary source for the historical details concerning which it gives information.[24]

There is a grain of truth in this principle. As Edward H. Carr has said, no document can tell us more than what the author of the document thought.[25] If Matthew, Mark, Luke, and John all report that Jesus was crucified, this does not prove he really was crucified, but only that these four men believed (or stated that they believed) he was. The same is true of information about current events. If I read an account of someone's death in a newspaper, that information is "secondary"—it has passed through the hands of reporters and editors who were not eyewitnesses of the event reported. But in spite of this I read a newspaper to gain information—not information about the "life situation" of newspaper reporters and editors, but information about the events those reporters and editors relate.

Most readers of the gospels do the same. Even though the gospel writers were not eyewitnesses of all the events they describe, they knew some of the original eyewitnesses, and we turn to their "secondary" reports, as we turn to the secondary reports in a newspaper, for information regarding what really happened.

The problem with the Wellhausen-Bultmann principle is that often "secondary" is taken to mean "inferior" or "unreliable," and "primary" is taken to mean "reliable." The information in the gospels about what Jesus said and did is regarded as "secondary," and therefore we cannot know what really happened; but the conjectures modern scholars make about the early Christian communities are based on "primary" evidence, and therefore we can know clearly what these communities were like. Skepticism about the gospel accounts of the ministry of Jesus goes hand in hand with a strange credulity about modern hypothetical reconstructions of the life and thought of the early Christians.

C. S. Lewis regarded the capacity of the radical to believe the incredible as being one of the distinctive marks of twentieth-century New Testament criticism.

---

[23]Ibid., 201-203.

[24]Rudolf Karl Bultmann, "The New Approach to the Synoptic Problem," in *Existence and Faith: Shorter Writings of Rudolf Bultmann*, trans. Schubert M. Ogden (London: Hodder & Stoughton, 1961; Cleveland/New York: World Pub. Co., 1960) 42 (USA 38).

[25]Edward Hallett Carr, *What Is History?* (Harmondsworth: Penguin Books; New York: Viking Penguin, 1964) 16.

Scholars have pointed out sources of difficulties that, in their opinion, make the gospel story as a whole impossible to believe; but they then go on, Lewis observed, to believe something far more incredible—that the real behavior and teaching of Christ came very rapidly to be misunderstood and misrepresented by his followers, and has been recovered or exhumed only by modern scholars. Lewis had heard this sort of claim made in other fields—Jowett's view that Plato had never been properly understood until the nineteenth century, or modern discoveries of what Shakespeare *really* meant—but to him it was fantastic:

> The idea that any man or writer should be opaque to those who lived in the same culture, spoke the same language, shared the same habitual imagery and unconscious assumptions, and yet be transparent to those who have none of these advantages, is in my opinion preposterous. There is an a priori improbability in it which almost no argument and no evidence could counterbalance.[26]

The Problem of Shared Presuppositions

Specialists are able to discuss their ideas only within a limited circle of people. They therefore tend to share the presuppositions of that circle. That their presuppositions are shared by their colleagues may give them a feeling of false security, and prevent them from seeing how odd those presuppositions appear to the world outside.

It may seem strange to talk about shared presuppositions when scholars spend so much time arguing among themselves. But it is possible for people to disagree about many things even though their presuppositions are the same. A case in point is the modern debate about structuralism.

According to Raymond F. Collins, some of the structuralists claim there is no valid method of literary analysis other than the structural one, and reject altogether the historical-critical method of biblical interpretation.[27] This might seem at first sight to indicate a complete break with the past. But rejection of the methodology of earlier critics does not necessarily imply rejection of their presuppositions. For example, Erhardt Güttgemanns has raised many questions about the methodology of the form critics; but he makes it plain that his quarrel is more with the methods and dogmatism of earlier scholars than with their basic assumptions:

---

[26]Lewis, *Christian Reflections,* 197-98.

[27]Raymond F. Collins, *Introduction to the New Testament* (New York: Doubleday, 1983) 256.

To avoid a possible misunderstanding of this work it should be stated expressly that the acceptance of oral tradition and also the assumption of "small units" as well as pre-Markan redactional compositions is not disputed here in the least. But the path to these "small units" and this tradition-history, up to the point of the "literary" gospel form, seems to me to be much less certain and more hypothetical than is generally recognized today.[28]

Gospel criticism in the twentieth century has tended increasingly to regard the gospels as evidence for what the early church believed, rather than for what Jesus actually said and did. This tendency can lead in either of two directions. In the opinion of some, the search for the prehistory of the gospel material is so hypothetical that it is not worth undertaking, and we should treat the gospels simply as literary compositions by their respective authors. In the opinion of others, the search for genuine sayings of Jesus beneath the veneer of early church interpretation is still worth pursuing despite the hypothetical nature of the results. Although these two approaches differ, they both start from the same standpoint. Neither of them takes seriously the view that the gospels are based on reliable eyewitness evidence, because it is presupposed that the scientific criticism of earlier generations has made such a view untenable.

The problem with presuppositions is not that they exist, but that all too often they are allowed to go unquestioned. We all have presuppositions of some sort, based on what we have learned and experienced in the past. Even the newborn baby emerges from the womb with some idea of what is good and what is bad.

Sherlock Holmes claimed to be able to approach problems with "an absolutely blank mind";[29] but in making this claim he deceived himself. His mind was no more blank than anyone else's. For instance, in attempting to solve the mystery of the Devil's Foot, he laid down this principle:

I take it, in the first place, that neither of us is prepared to admit diabolical intrusions into the affairs of men. Let us begin by ruling that entirely out of our minds.[30]

Holmes did not provide evidence to support this assumption—nor could he. It is no more possible to give scientific proof of the nonexistence of diabolical powers than to give scientific proof of their existence. In presupposing an unproved hypothesis, Holmes revealed how far he was from having the absolutely blank mind he thought he had.

---

[28]Güttgemanns, *Candid Questions*, 105.

[29]Arthur Conan Doyle, "The Adventure of the Cardboard Box," in *His Last Bow* (New York: Viking Penguin; London: Penguin Books, 1981) 51.

[30]Doyle, "The Adventure of the Devil's Foot," in ibid., 162-63.

No student of the New Testament approaches it with a blank mind. In his *Method in Theology* Bernard Lonergan discusses the question, How is a critic to understand the mind and work of another writer? One answer that has been suggested is what Lonergan calls "the principle of the empty head." According to this principle, if critics are not to read into the text what is not there, they must drop all preconceptions and simply let the author's text speak for itself. "In brief, the less one knows, the better an exegete one will be."[31]

People who argue in this way, says Lonergan, are recognizing a real difficulty—the fact that critics sometimes attribute to an author ideas the author did not express—but their solution is wrong. The ability of critics to understand an author depends not on the emptiness of their heads but on the breadth of their experience, intelligence, and judgment. What a critic needs is not a blank mind but a broad mind, filled with such a variety of knowledge and experience that new facts and experiences can be fitted into their appropriate place.

The problem is that the breadth of anyone's mind is limited. Because of the explosion of knowledge in the twentieth century, the amount of knowledge one individual is able to grasp becomes every day a smaller and smaller proportion of the total knowledge available. In this situation the alternative to a blank mind can easily become, not a broad mind, but a narrow mind. We limit our thinking to areas we know something about, and give to our limited knowledge a universal application it does not deserve. Narrowing the scope of an investigation becomes as necessary to research as blinkers are to a skittish horse.

Sherlock Holmes, by excluding the possibility of diabolical intrusions, gained two ends: he narrowed the field of investigation to those areas he believed to be worthwhile; and he established a common basis upon which to discuss the case with his colleague, since both shared the same presupposition. These are things that scholars need to do. They do not want to waste precious time in disproving ideas already disproved, or in proving again ideas already established. Moreover, since all published work is intended for a particular audience, they need to find a common ground with that audience, so the ideas they have in common can form a basis upon which to build ideas that are new.

This narrowing process has obvious advantages; it also has obvious dangers. Scholars write mainly for academic audiences. They can easily come to believe that, because their audience shares their presuppositions, those presuppositions must be true. If people outside their field of specialization find it difficult to accept the conclusions built upon those presuppositions, that is taken as an indication that those outsiders are unwilling to accept the truth.

In the case of the New Testament, it has often been noted that there is a gulf between the pulpit and the pew—between the ideas put forward by preachers on

---

[31]Bernard Lonergan, *Method in Theology* (London: Darton, Longman & Todd, 1972) 157.

the authority of the best modern scholarship, and the beliefs of those who sit in a pew and listen. This gulf is sometimes regarded as a sign of the narrow-mindedness of those in the pew, who are not open to the truth as it comes to them, via the pulpit, from the theological specialists. But it could equally be a sign of the narrow-mindedness of the specialists, who do not realize that the people in the pew may have a broader experience and knowledge than they have, and may therefore have also a more balanced judgment.

The Advantages of the Nonspecialist

(1) *It is easier for the nonspecialist to use historical imagination.* A great deal of New Testament study is concerned with what R. G. Collingwood called "imaginative reconstruction of the past"[32]—imagining what the early church was like, and how the New Testament writers felt and worked. This is the method advocated by the great detective Sherlock Holmes:

> "You'll get results, Inspector, by always putting yourself in the other fellow's place, and thinking what you would do yourself. It takes some imagination, but it pays."[33]

Two hundred years ago J. J. Wettstein advised students of the New Testament to use this method:

> If you wish to get a thorough and complete understanding of the books of the New Testament, put yourself in the place of those to whom they were first delivered by the apostles as a legacy. Transfer yourself in thought to that time and that area where they were first read. . . .[34]

Since Wettstein's time there have been many attempts to imagine the thought processes of Matthew, Mark, Luke, John, Paul, and the early Christians as a whole. One problem, however, is that most of these reconstructions are made by academic scholars; and in trying to imagine the thought processes of early Christians, academic scholars are at a grave disadvantage.

---

[32]Robin George Collingwood, *The Idea of History* (Oxford: Oxford University Press, 1946) 247.

[33]Arthur Conan Doyle, "The Adventure of the Retired Colourman," in *The Case-Book of Sherlock Holmes* (London: John Murray, 1934) 318.

[34]Johann Jakob Wettstein, *Novum Testamentum Graecum editionis receptae cum lectionibus variantibus . . .* , 2 vols. (Amsterdam: Ex Officina Dommeriana, 1751/1752), from vol. 2 as quoted in Werner Georg Kümmel, *The New Testament: The History of the Investigation of Its Problems,* trans. S. McLean Gilmour and Howard C. Kee (London: SCM Press; Nashville/New York: Abingdon Press, 1972) 50.

The early Christians were not, on the whole, well educated. When Peter and John dared to dispute theology with the Jerusalem pundits, people were amazed, because Peter and John were "unlearned and ignorant men" (Acts 4:13 KJV). The Corinthian church, as we noted earlier, did not contain many upper-class people who could afford a good education, and the intellectual Paul had to adapt his style to their level. Therefore, in trying to imagine the thoughts of an early Christian, the twentieth-century academic faces a double problem—not only the culture gap between the first century and the twentieth century, but also the culture gap between the intellectual and the nonintellectual.

Perhaps it is this latter culture gap that can explain one of the curiosities of modern scholarship—the belief that early Christians, because many of them were not well educated, would not be able to distinguish between secondhand evidence and eyewitness evidence. This belief is a product of intellectual culture. Intellectuals are aware that their knowledge is superior to that of other people, but do not always realize how limited are the areas in which that is true. They may be tempted to confuse lack of education with lack of intelligence. "Ordinary" people, on the other hand, know instinctively that early Christians were people like themselves. They know from their experience that to give extra value to the evidence of an eyewitness is not to be modern or scientific, but to be human.

The use of historical imagination is of special importance when employing the argument from incredibility. According to this argument, the gospel accounts of various events cannot be believed because the behavior of the early disciples was "incredible." In discussions of this sort, specialist scholars tend to be logical, and to expect of the early disciples a logical pattern of behavior. By contrast, ordinary people find it easier to credit the disciples with illogical behavior because they know that their own behavior is often illogical.

There are two feeding miracles in Mark's gospel—the feeding of the five thousand in chapter 6 and the feeding of the four thousand in chapter 8. According to Dennis E. Nineham, it is now "generally accepted" that these are alternative accounts of a single incident. One reason for this belief is that, if the disciples had already been through the experience described in chapter 6, "it is incredible that they should have been so dull and uncomprehending" as Mark says they were in chapter 8.[35]

This kind of argument is subjective at the best of times, and in the case of the feeding miracles seems unusually weak. What the disciples did, according to Mark 8:4, was to ask the question, "Where in this desert can anyone find enough food to feed all these people?" Nineham assumes that, having once experienced the miraculous activity of Jesus, they should never have doubted it again. But in real

---

[35]Dennis Eric Nineham, *The Gospel of Saint Mark,* Pelican Gospel Commentaries (Harmondsworth: Penguin Books; Baltimore: Penguin Books, 1963) 205-206.

life, as C. E. B. Cranfield comments, "even mature Christians (which the disciples at that time certainly were not) do often doubt the power of God after they have had signal expression of it."[36] The unbelief of the disciples is a recurring theme in the gospels. Whether or not we find it incredible depends on our understanding of human nature in general, and our ability to enter into the minds of twelve ordinary people caught up in, and often puzzled by, the extraordinary actions of their extraordinary leader.

The behavior of the disciples after the resurrection was equally illogical. Is it credible that Mary Magdalene should think the body of Jesus to have been stolen if she had just heard an angel declare that God had raised him from death? Or perhaps we should put the question another way: Is a scholar sitting calmly at his or her desk the best-qualified person to imagine the thought processes of someone like Mary Magdalene—confused, bewildered, tired after a sleepless night, struggling to cope with an emotional crisis?

When scholars lay down what early Christians were capable of doing, they are really stating what they themselves are capable of believing. In his review of Walter Laqueur's *The Terrible Secret* (which describes people's reactions to the mass extermination of Jews during World War II) Hugh Trevor-Roper commented on the fact that those faced with the evidence found it impossible to believe. Why was this? Partly because governments suppressed what evidence they could for political reasons. Partly because of a form-critical type of argument from analogy—stories of German atrocities during World War I had been grossly exaggerated; therefore the atrocity story as a form must always be exaggerated. But mainly for another reason:

> The greatest obstacle to belief lay not in present politics or past experience; it arose—and this is the most interesting part of Mr. Laqueur's work—from the internal limits of human belief. In Western Europe, in the full light and freedom of the 20th century, men simply could not bring themselves to believe in such atrocities.[37]

The events described in the New Testament are of a different order to the actions of the Nazis; but they are just as contrary to most people's normal experience, and may therefore be just as hard for twentieth-century Europeans or Americans to believe. Those who declare which of these events are possible and which are impossible tend to reflect the "internal limits of human belief" in theo-

[36]Charles E. B. Cranfield, *The Gospel according to Saint Mark: An Introduction and Commentary,* Cambridge Greek Testament Commentary (Cambridge: Cambridge University Press, 1963) 205.

[37]Hugh R. Trevor-Roper, review of Walter Laqueur, *The Terrible Secret* (London: Weidenfeld, 1980) *The Listener* (1 January 1981): 19.

logical circles in the twentieth century rather than inside knowledge of what happened in the first century.

(2) *The nonspecialist's expertise is practical, not theoretical.* In his presidential address to the American Historical Association in 1931, Carl Becker took as his subject "Everyman his own historian." Becker described what happens when Mr. Everyman needs to pay his coal bill. From his Private Record Office (his vest pocket) he takes a book in manuscript, turns to page 23, and reads, "December 29, pay Smith's coal bill." He goes to Smith's office and is told that Smith did not have the kind of coal he wanted, and turned the order over to Brown. He goes to Brown's office and pays the bill. On returning home he examines another collection of documents and discovers Brown's bill. In this process, Becker observed, Mr. Everyman performed all the essential operations involved in historical research—recalling things said and done, examining documents, comparing the texts critically when there was a conflicting report, and eventually formulating a definitive picture of a series of historical events. If he had undertaken these researches to write a book instead of to pay a bill, no one would think of denying that he was a historian.[38]

All of us, in the course of our everyday life, practice critical thinking. We listen to salespersons, politicians, and gossiping neighbors, and learn by experience who can be trusted. That is why important decisions in a court of law, such as deciding whether or not someone has committed murder, are made by a jury of ordinary people. Technical experts take part in the trial, and give evidence about fingerprints and similar matters; but the jury system assumes that, in deciding whether or not a witness is reliable, and whether an accused person is innocent or guilty, the judgment of the nonspecialist is likely to be sound.

One reason for this is that the nonspecialist tends to be guided by common sense rather than by logical principles, and is therefore willing to take the risk of believing what cannot be logically proved. This commonsense approach is of vital importance in study of the New Testament. The Christian faith depends on the historical facts of the life, death, and resurrection of Jesus Christ. These facts can never be proved in the same way that a mathematical theorem can be proved. But neither can most of the things we believe and rely on in daily life. I believe a railroad timetable, the word of a newspaper, or the word of a neighbor, even though none of these can be "proved." As R. W. Hepburn has said, "no amount of subtlety can provide historicity without the *risks* of historicity."[39] Some have argued that these risks can be avoided by basing Christian faith, not on historical facts,

----

[38]Carl Lotus Becker, *Everyman His Own Historian* (New York: F. S. Crofts & Co., 1935) 235-39.

[39]Ronald W. Hepburn, *Christianity and Paradox* (London: Watts, 1958) 110.

but on abstract ideas. This approach jettisons the heart of Christianity, and leads, in Hepburn's words, to "a sense of false security, an illusion that the risks of history can be and have been eliminated."[40]

There will always be areas, such as textual criticism of the Greek text, that require specialist knowledge. But when it comes to basic questions such as "What is a parable?", "Did Jesus perform miracles?", "Could the gospel writers distinguish fact from fiction?", "Did Jesus rise from the dead?"—in deciding these questions the theories of the professionals need to be both assessed and corrected by the common sense of ordinary people.

In one of his detective stories H. R. F. Keating describes how a charwoman, Mrs. Craggs, was able to detect a crime that had baffled the experts. At the Borough Museum where she worked the celebrated *Golden Venus* was on a week's loan exhibition. Mrs. Craggs knew from dusting it that it had been replaced by a fake. The assistant curator, Mr. Slythe, disagreed. He could see in the replica "the unmistakable patina of age." But Mrs. Craggs could tell by the touch. She had dusted the original five times, and knew the feel of it as well as she knew the back of her hand. So she searched until she found the original hidden behind some loose tiles in the wall.[41]

Mr. Slythe was an expert, well qualified to speak about many aspects of art; but in determining what was genuine and what was secondary, Mrs. Craggs was also an expert, with an expertise born of personal experience. There is a similar variety of expertise in the field of New Testament interpretation. The New Testament writers were describing what they had "touched and handled" of the word of life (1 John 1). Christians today who have come into personal contact with that word have a "feel" for what is genuine. This "feel" is not infallible. It needs to be tested just as rigorously as do the theories of the professional scholars. But it constitutes a kind of practical expertise the theoretical experts ignore at their peril.

---

[40]Ibid., 125.

[41]Henry Raymond Fitzwalter Keating, "The Five Senses of Mrs. Craggs," in *Ellery Queen's Murdercade* (New York: Random House, 1975) 238-61.

Appendix

A Reappraisal of Rudolf Bultmann in the Light of Form Criticism*

The second half of the twenty-first century has seen a revival of "form criticism." This method of criticism was widely used by New Testament scholars in the twentieth century. They would take a story or saying in the gospels, analyze the "form" in which it was written, and deduce from that analysis how and why the story or saying was passed on and modified in the early church.

By the end of the twentieth century, form criticism of the gospels was no longer practiced. Scholars had come to realize how little was known about the period with which gospel form criticism was concerned—the years between the resurrection of Jesus and the writing of the gospels. The form critics were seen to have worked largely by guesswork. Form criticism became discredited as a scholarly technique.

In recent years, however, form criticism has been revived in a different area. It is now used as a tool for analyzing, not the New Testament itself, but the writings of twentieth-century New Testament scholars. This is a more fruitful use of the tool because we know a great deal about the "life situation" (*Sitz im Leben*) of twentieth-century scholars. We have, for example, the recent study by Professor Dee in which he analyzes that most characteristic of twentieth-century scholarly art forms, the doctoral dissertation.[1] In this article I wish to contribute to this

---

*This article is preprinted by kind permission from the *Journal of Twentieth Century Studies* 90/3 (January 2090): 361-65.

[1] P. H. Dee, *Ecclesiastes 12:11-12 and the Twentieth Century* (Beijing: University Publishing Houses Ltd., 2080).

developing area of research by means of a form-critical analysis of a passage from *The Gospel of John* by Rudolf Bultmann.[2]

The subject matter of this passage is the miracle of changing water into wine as recorded in John 2:1-11. Bultmann believed the gospel writer took this story from a previous written source:

> The *source* [*Quelle*] counted this as the first miracle. It is easy to see why it put it at the beginning of its collection; for it is an epiphany miracle. There are no analogies with it in the old tradition of Jesus-stories, and in comparison with them it appears strange and alien to us. There can be no doubt that the story has been taken over from heathen legend and ascribed to Jesus. In fact the motif of the story, the changing of the water into wine, is a typical motif of the Dionysus legend. In the legend this miracle is the miracle of the epiphany of the god, and was therefore dated on the day of the Dionysus Feast, that is on the night of the 5th to 6th of January. This relationship was still understood in the Early Church, which saw the Feast of Christ's Baptism as his epiphany and celebrated it on the 6th of January. Equally it held that the 6th of January was the date of the marriage at Cana.[3]

The key sentence in this passage is, "There can be no doubt that the story has been taken over from heathen legend and ascribed to Jesus." Professor Crochip has classified this sentence as a DS (Dogmatic Statement). Crochip lists three categories of the DS: the DS^p, Dogmatic Statement Based on Presupposition; the DS^g, Dogmatic Statement Based on Guesswork; and the DS^{ie}, Dogmatic Statement Based on Insufficient Evidence. Common to all three categories are two characteristics of the DS, namely,

---

[2]Rudolf Karl Bultmann (1884-1976), *Das Evangelium des Johannes*, Kritisch-exegetischer Kommentar über das Neue Testament, 2nd ed. (Göttingen: Vandenhoeck & Ruprecht, 1950; [1]1941-1947); *Ergänzungsheft* (1950). ET: *The Gospel of John. A Commentary*, trans. George R. Beasley-Murray (Oxford: Blackwell; Philadelphia: Westminster, 1971).

[3]*The Gospel of John. A Commentary* (1971) 118-19. The original text is as follows.

Die Quelle hat dieses Wunder als erstes gezählt. Dass sie es an den Anfang ihrer Sammlung gestellt hat, ist sehr begreiflich; denn es ist ein Epiphaniewunder. In der alten Tradition der Jesus-Geschichten hat es keine Analogien und befremdet im Vergleich mit ihnen. Zweifellos ist die Geschichte aus heidnischer Legende übernommen und auf Jesus übertragen worden. In der Tat ist das Motiv der Geschichte, die Verwandlung des Wassers in Wein, ein typisches Motiv der Dionysos-Legende, in der dieses Wunder eben das Wunder der Epiphanie des Gottes ist und deshalb auf den Zeitpunkt des Dionysos-Festes, nämlich die Nacht vom 5. auf den 6. Januar, datiert wird. In der alten Kirche ist diese Verwandtschaft noch verstanden worden, wenn man das Fest der Taufe Christi als seine Epiphanie auf den 6. Januar setzte, und ebenso, wenn man den 6. Januar für den Tag der Hochzeit von Kana hielt. —*Das Evangelium des Johannes*, 83

a. an introductory formula stating there can be no other interpretation, and
b. failure to mention the other interpretations that were available.[4]

These two characteristics are clearly present in the key sentence:

a. the introductory formula—"there can be no doubt that . . . "
b. failure to mention the other interpretations which could be found in commentaries on the same story in contemporary authors.

Scholars disagree as to which category of DS this key sentence represents. Some classify it as a DS[p]. They point out that Bultmann's rejection of one possible explanation of the story (namely, that the miracle actually happened) was a result of his presupposition about miracles. As is well known, Bultmann was under the influence of the twentieth-century "modern man" mythology. He therefore rejected the possibility of any miracle that could not be explained by the limited scientific knowledge of his day.

Others classify the sentence as a DS[ie]. They claim that Bultmann did bring forward evidence, though not sufficient to prove his point. This evidence was fourfold: (1) the miracle story differed from the miracle stories in the Synoptic Gospels; (2) the story appeared strange and alien to twentieth-century Europeans; (3) the motif of the story appeared also in legends about the Greek god Dionysus; and (4) the early church observed the night of the feast of Dionysus as the Feast of the Epiphany and as the date of the marriage at Cana.

None of these statements, however, can properly be called evidence for the origin of the story. Certainly there is a parallel between the gospel story and the Dionysus legend; but a parallel proves nothing about origins. Bultmann's DS was, it would seem, a guess. Of the many possible ways of explaining the origin of the story, this was the one that appealed to him. We should therefore classify it as a DS[g].

In the course of the twenty-first century there has been much discussion of the Bultmannian DS as a literary form. Scholars have understood the significance of the form in three ways.

1. *The literal interpretation.* According to the literal interpretation all Bultmann's statements were intended as statements of fact. When he wrote "there can be no doubt" he literally meant *there can be no doubt*. The problem with this interpretation is that in Bultmann's day there both could be and was doubt.

Consider, for example, the commentary of C. K. Barrett.[5] Barrett, like Bultmann, referred to the legendary power of Dionysus to change water into wine, but

---

[4]M. I. Crochip, *Computer Analysis of Twentieth-Century New Testament Scholars* (London: Oxbridge Megaversity Press, 2075) 616.

[5]Charles Kingsley Barrett, *The Gospel according to St John. An Introduction with Commentary and Notes on the Greek Text* (London: S.P.C.K., 1955) 157-58.

he also pointed out that the Jewish writer Philo referred to the Logos as the wine-giver. In Barrett's opinion, John might have followed the Jewish precedent of Philo; or "it is even conceivable that the miracle story had a non-Christian origin" (157); or again, the story could be related to the synoptic tradition, with its references to wine and wedding feasts. "The Johannine narrative may have simply been made up out of these elements, or John may have taken an already existing story and . . . used it to bring out these points" (157-58).

Barrett's comments exemplify the normal "form" of a twentieth-century scholarly commentary. The characteristics of this form were (a) an examination of various possible interpretations and (b) a refusal to dogmatize where the evidence was inconclusive. By contrast, Bultmann's commentary contains only a Dogmatic Statement of *one* possible hypothesis. It seems incredible that a scientific twentieth-century scholar should have intended literally a statement of this kind.

2. *The existential interpretation.* The existential interpretation is based on the distinction that Bultmann drew elsewhere between "Historie" (the bare facts of history) and "Geschichte" (*meaningful* history). According to this interpretation, Bultmann's Dogmatic Statement was "Geschichte" and could be paraphrased as follows.

> The assumption that this story has been taken over from heathen legend gives us today a basis for existential decision making about which we can have no doubt.

Professor Ampelophilos has suggested that the decision making Bultmann had in mind concerned the wine industry, so vital to the economy of Germany in the twentieth century. Ampelophilos thinks the wine industry may have been under threat at that period, because of social problems connected with alcoholism. If the church of Bultmann's day were to recognize that the gospel story was dependent on a pagan wine festival, it could then make an existential decision to support more actively the traditional wine festivals of Germany, many of which had similar pagan origins.

However true this may be, most scholars regard the views of Professor Ampelophilos as eccentric. But it is not easy to think of any other existential decision that could have been in Bultmann's mind when he made his Dogmatic Statement.

3. *The criminological interpretation.* Advocates of the criminological interpretation point out the many similarities between twentieth-century New Testament scholars and the heroes of the detective stories so popular at that period. Like the fictional detectives, the scholars spoke with great authority. They were able to show up other investigators for the fools they were. They alone could discern, amid the mass of evidence, those clues that were significant. They had disciples who wrote theses under their direction, just as the detectives had disciples (often

called "Watsons") who admired and reported their methods of detection. Many critics therefore regard the work of Bultmann as belonging to the *Gattung* of detective fiction.

We should not underestimate the psychological importance of the detective story for Christians in the twentieth century. At a time when the traditional sources of infallibility, the church and the Bible, were under increasing attack, the illusion of infallibility created by the great fictional detectives was very comforting. It is significant that many detective stories were written by leading religious authors, such as G. K. Chesterton and Dorothy Sayers. For Christians in need of reassurance, the Bultmannian Dogmatic Statement may well have performed a psychological function similar to that of the detective story.

Nevertheless, there was one decisive difference between Bultmann and the detectives. The best detectives always based their conclusions upon sound evidence. If they did resort to guesswork, their guesses were not made public until they had been objectively confirmed. Their pronouncements were thus quite unlike the DS which, in its characteristic Bultmannian form, was based either on insufficient evidence or on none at all.

4. *The gelotological interpretation.* Previous attempts to analyze the form of the Bultmannian Dogmatic Statement having proved unconvincing, I wish to adduce a twentieth-century parallel that, I believe, can throw new light on this problem. It forms part of an essay by a later contemporary of Bultmann, Frank Muir.

> In my opinion the decline of the British nation as a great power is directly connected with the decline in our consumption of boiled pudding.
>
> It is an undeniable fact that our nation began to lose its preeminence at the same time as the good, old-fashioned steamed suet pudding fell into desuetude.[6]

The characteristic marks of the DS are both present in this passage:

a. the introductory formula—"it is an undeniable fact . . . "
b. no mention of any alternative explanation of the phenomenon under discussion (the decline of the British nation).

Professor Ernest Chuckle, Professor of Risible Science at Aberdeen University, in his study of humorous writing in the twentieth century, puts Frank Muir in the category of "sit-down comics."[7] These were comedians who appeared on television and took part in intellectual games. One of the requirements of a sit-

---

[6]Frank Muir and Denis Norden, *Upon My Word* (London: Eyre, Methuen, 1974) 40.

[7]Ernest Chuckle, *Twentieth-Century Gelotology* (Aberdeen: Aberdeen University Press, 2079) 53.

down comic was to keep what was known as a "straight face"[8]—to make statements purporting to be statements of fact without betraying their falsity by facial expression. This style of speaking and writing, which belonged originally to the playing of intellectual games, was then extended to other fields.

The twentieth century is often called "the age of sport." Sport was the major preoccupation of many people in that century. More pages in newspapers were devoted to sport than to any other subject. It would therefore be natural for an academic writer of that period, who wished to present his material in a form the general public would understand, to employ the "sporting" style of sit-down comedy. The problem for us in the twenty-first century is that we do not instinctively appreciate this style of writing. Only when the literary form of a twentieth-century work has been determined can the modern reader discern whether its statements are intended literally or humorously.

In my opinion, the parallel between the method of argument of Bultmann and that of Muir is so close that we must regard their writings as belonging to the same literary genre. I hope that, when this is recognized, the works of Bultmann, which are now little read except by researchers in twentieth-century studies, will be appreciated for what they are—masterpieces of twentieth-century comedy.

---

[8]The origin of this phrase is obscure. Straightness, a predicate of lineal progression, is not a natural description of a face. It may be, as Dr. Wright has suggested, the phrase is a corruption of "strait face," that is, narrow face (U. Speke Wright, *Applied Orthoglottics* [New York: Lingua Press, 2070] 248). Or it may be an example of the inaccuracy of language characteristic of the primitive, precomputerized culture of the 20th century.

Bibliography

Auerbach, Erich. *Mimesis: The Representation of Reality in Western Literature.* Trans. Willard R. Trask. Princeton: Princeton University Press, 1953.

Baird, Joseph Arthur. *Audience Criticism and the Historical Jesus.* Philadelphia: Westminster Press, 1969.

Barclay, William. *The Letters to the Galatians and Ephesians.* Daily Study Bible. Second edition. Edinburgh: Saint Andrew Press; Philadelphia: Westminster Press, 1958.

Barrett, Charles Kingsley. *The Gospel according to St. John: An Introduction with Commentary and Notes on the Greek Text.* London: S.P.C.K., 1955.

Beardslee, William A. *Literary Criticism of the New Testament.* Philadelphia: Fortress Press, 1969.

Beare, Francis Wright. *The First Epistle of Peter.* Second edition. Oxford: Basil Blackwell, 1961 ([1]1958; [3]1970).

Becker, Carl Lotus. *Everyman His Own Historian.* New York: F. S. Crofts & Co., 1935.

Beecham, Sir Thomas. Essay (c1959) introducing Handel's *Messiah* on RCA record set GL 02444(3). London: RCA Records, 1977.

Berger, Peter L. *A Rumor of Angels.* New York: Doubleday, 1969.

Bloch, Marc. *The Historian's Craft.* Manchester: Manchester University Press, 1954.

de Bono, Edward. *The Use of Lateral Thinking.* London: Penguin Books, 1971. (London: Jonathan Cape, 1967.)

Bowden, John. "Great Expectations? The New Testament Critic and His Audience." In *What about the New Testament?,* ed. Morna D. Hooker and Colin J. A. Hickling, 1-12. London: SCM Press, 1975.

Braaten, Carl E. *History and Hermeneutics.* New Directions in Theology Today 2. Philadelphia: Westminster Press; London: Lutterworth Press, 1968.

Brooks, Peter. *Communicating Conviction.* London: Epworth Press, 1983.

Bultmann, Rudolf Karl. *The Gospel of John: A Commentary.* Trans. George R. Beasley-Murray. Oxford: Blackwell; Philadelphia: Westminster, 1971. Original: *Das Evangelium des Johannes.* Second and thoroughly revised edition (ii. durchgesehene Auflage), with *Ergänzungsheft* (bound separately). Kritisch-exegetischer Kommentar über das Neue Testament. Göttingen: Vandenhoeck & Ruprecht, 1950; [1]1940-1947.

_____. *Die Erforschung der synoptischen Evangelien.* Giessen: Töpelmann, 1930. ET: *Form Criticism.* Trans. F. C. Grant. Chicago: Willett, Clark, 1934.

_____. *Geschichte der synoptischen Tradition*. Göttingen: Vandenhoek & Ruprecht, 1921. ET: *The History of the Synoptic Tradition*. Trans. John Marsh. Oxford: Basil Blackwell; New York and Evanston: Harper & Row, 1963.

_____. "The New Approach to the Synoptic Problem." In *Existence and Faith: Shorter Writings of Rudolf Bultmann*, trans. Schubert M. Ogden, 35-54 (USA); 39-66 (British). Cleveland/New York: World Publishing Co./Meridian Books, 1960; London: Hodder & Stoughton, 1961. (Pagination in British edition differs from that of the USA edition.) Original: *The Journal of Religion* 6 (1926): 337-62.

Butterfield, Herbert. *The Discontinuities between the Generations in History*. Cambridge: Cambridge University Press, 1971.

Caird, George Bradford. "Do Computers Count.[*sic*]" *Expository Times* 76 (1964/1965): 176.

Carr, Edward Hallett. *What Is History?* Harmondsworth: Penguin Books; New York: Viking Penguin, 1964. (London: Macmillan, 1961.)

Carson, Donald A. *Exegetical Fallacies*. Grand Rapids MI: Baker Book House, 1984.

Chadwick, Henry. "Ephesians." In *Peake's Commentary on the Bible*, Matthew Black, gen. ed. Sunbury-on-Thames: Thomas Nelson & Sons Ltd.; New York: Nelson, 1962.

Chambers English Dictionary. London and New York: W. & R. Chambers Ltd. and Cambridge University Press, 1988.

Chambers, Edmund Kerchever. *Shakespearean Gleanings*. London: Oxford University Press, 1944.

Chesterton, Gilbert Keith. *The Club of Queer Trades*. Beaconsfield, England: Darwen Finlayson, 1960 (1905).

_____. *The Incredulity of Father Brown*. Harmondsworth, England: Penguin Books, 1958. (London: Collins, 1926.)

_____. *Orthodoxy*. London: Collins, 1961. (The Bodley Head, 1908.)

Christie, Agatha. *An Autobiography*. London: Collins, 1977.

_____. *Dead Man's Folly*. London: Collins, 1973.

_____. *Parker Pyne Investigates*. London: Collins, 1962 (¹1934).

_____. *Towards Zero*. London: Pan Books Ltd., 1948. (London: Collins, 1944.)

Clark, George Sidney Roberts Kitson. *The Critical Historian*. London: Heinemann; New York: Basic Books, 1967.

Clarke, Arthur Charles. *Profiles of the Future*. New York: Harper & Row; London: Victor Gollancz, 1962.

Collingwood, Robin George. *Essays in the Philosophy of History*. Austin: University of Texas Press, 1965.

_____. *The Idea of History*. Oxford: Oxford University Press, 1946.

Collins, Raymond F. *Introduction to the New Testament*. London: SCM Press; Garden City NY: Doubleday, 1983.

Cranfield, Charles E. B. *The Gospel according to Saint Mark: An Introduction and Commentary*. Cambridge Greek Testament Commentary. Cambridge: Cambridge University Press, 1963 (¹1959; reprint with supplementary notes, 1977).

Crompton, Richmal. *William Carries On*. London: Collins, 1972. (London: George Newnes, 1942.)

_____. *William the Detective*. London: Collins, 1971. (London: George Newnes.)

_____. *William the Gangster*. London: Collins, 1971. (London: George Newnes.)

Crossan, John Dominic. *In Parables: The Challenge of the Historical Jesus*. San Francisco and New York: Harper & Row, 1973.

Deissmann, Adolf. *Light from the Ancient East: The New Testament and the Newly Discovered Texts from the Hellenistic-Roman World*. Trans. Lionel R. M. Strachan. London: Hodder & Stoughton, 1910.

Dickens, Charles. *Barnaby Rudge*. London: Chapman and Hall, n.d. ([1]1841).

Dodd, Charles Harold. *The Parables of the Kingdom*. Revised edition. London: Collins, 1961. New York: Charles Scribner's Sons, 1961. (Pagination in the U.S.A. edition differs from that of the British edition.) (London: James Nisbet & Co., 1935. [2]1936; [3]1936; [4]1948.)

Doty, William G. *Contemporary New Testament Interpretation*. Englewood Cliffs NJ: Prentice-Hall, 1972.

Doyle, Arthur Conan. *The Case-Book of Sherlock Holmes*. London: John Murray, 1934. Cited: "The Adventure of the Retired Colourman," 299-320.

_____. *The Complete Sherlock Holmes Long Stories*. London: John Murray and Jonathan Cape, 1977. Cited: "The Hound of the Baskervilles" and "The Valley of Fear."

_____. *The Final Adventures of Sherlock Holmes*. London: W. H. Allen, 1981.

_____. *His Last Bow*. New York: Viking Penguin; London: Penguin Books, 1981 (1917). Cited: "The Adventure of the Cardboard Box," 39-61, and "The Adventure of the Devil's Foot," 153-80.

_____. *The Memoirs of Sherlock Holmes*. London: Penguin Books; New York: Viking Penguin Inc., 1950. Cited: "Silver Blaze," 7-34.

Drury, John H. *The Parables in the Gospels*. London: S.P.C.K., 1985.

Dunn, James D. G. *Unity and Diversity in the New Testament*. London: SCM Press, 1977.

Durrell, Gerald. *My Family and Other Animals*. Harmondsworth: Penguin Books, 1959. (London: Rupert Hart-Davis, 1956.)

Edgar, David. "In Defense of Drama-Documentaries." In *The Listener*, 1 January 1981, 10-11.

Eliot, George. "Janet's Repentance." In *Scenes of Clerical Life*, 191-334. London: Oxford University Press/Clarendon Press, 1985.

Ellis, Edward Earle. *Paul's Use of the Old Testament*. Grand Rapids MI: Eerdmans; Edinburgh: Oliver & Boyd, 1957.

Evans, Christopher F. *Queen or Cinderella?* Durham: University of Durham, 1960.

Fornara, Charles William. *The Nature of History in Ancient Greece and Rome*. Berkeley: University of California Press, 1983.

Frankl, Victor E. "Reductionism and Nihilism." In *Beyond Reductionism*, ed. A. Koestler and J. R. Smythies. London, 1969.

Freeman, Richard Austin. *The Red Thumb Mark*. Bath: Lythway Press, n.d. (London: Collingwood Bros., 1907.)

Frye, Roland Mushat. "A Literary Perspective for the Criticism of the Gospels." In *Jesus and Man's Hope*, Pittsburgh Festival on the Gospels 1970, vol. 2 (Perspective 2), ed. Donald G. Miller and Dikran Y. Hadidian, 193-221. Pittsburgh: Pittsburgh Theological Seminary, 1971.

Fuller, Reginald Horace. *A Critical Introduction to the New Testament*. London: Gerald Duckworth and Co. Ltd., 1966.

al-Faruqi, Isma'il R. "The Concept and Practice of Christian Mission." *International Review of Missions* 65 (October 1976): 386.

Gardner, Helen. *Literary Studies*. Oxford: Oxford University Press, 1967.

Gattégno, Jean. *Lewis Carroll: Fragments of a Looking-Glass*. Trans. Rosemary Sheed. New York: Crowell, 1976; London: Allen & Unwin, 1977.

Geisel, Theodor Seuss. *The Dr. Seuss Story Book*. London: Collins, 1979.

Grenfell, Joyce. *George—Don't Do That. . . .* London: Futura Publications Ltd., 1978. (London: Macmillan, 1977.)

Güttgemanns, Erhardt. *Candid Questions Concerning Gospel Form Criticism*. Trans. William G. Doty. Pittsburgh: Pickwick Press, 1979.

Hacker, Andrew. *Political Theory: Philosophy, Ideology, Science*. New York: Macmillan, 1961.

Hanson, Anthony Tyrrell. "The Quandary of Historical Scepticism." In *Vindications*, ed A. T. Hanson, 74-102. London: SCM Press, 1966.

Harbage, Alfred. *Conceptions of Shakespeare*. Cambridge MA: Harvard University Press, 1966.

Harrison, George Bagshawe. Introduction to *The Tempest*. In *The Works of William Shakespeare*. Volume 2. London: William Clowes & Sons Ltd., 1934.

Harvey, Van Austin. *The Historian and the Believer*. New York: Macmillan, 1966; London: SCM Press, 1967.

Hengel, Martin. *Acts and the History of Earliest Christianity*. Trans. John Bowden. London: SCM Press, 1979; Philadelphia: Fortress Press, 1980.

——————. *Jews, Greeks, and Barbarians*. Trans. John Bowden. Philadelphia: Fortress Press; London: SCM Press, 1980.

——————. *Judaism and Hellenism: Studies in Their Encounter in Palestine during the Early Hellenistic Period*. Two volumes. Trans. John Bowden. London: SCM Press, 1974; Philadelphia: Fortress Press, 1981.

Hepburn, Ronald W. *Christianity and Paradox*. London: Watts, 1958.

Hooker, Morna Dorothy. "In His Own Image?" In *What about the New Testament*, ed. M. D. Hooker and Colin J. A. Hickling, 28-44. London: SCM Press, 1975.

——————. "On Using the Wrong Tool." *Theology 35 (1972): 570-81*.

Hooker, Morna Dorothy, and Colin J. A. Hickling, eds. *What about the New Testament*. London: SCM Press, 1975.

Housman, Alfred Edward. *The Confines of Criticism*. Cambridge: Cambridge University Press, 1969.

—————. *M. Manilii Astronomicon I*. Cambridge: Cambridge University Press, 1937.

—————. *Selected Prose*. Cambridge: Cambridge University Press, 1961.

Huck, Albert. *Synopsis of the First Three Gospels*. Ninth edition revised by Hans Lietzmann. English edition by Frank Leslie Cross. New York: American Bible Society, 1936ff. Oxford: Basil Blackwell, 1951ff.

Jowett, Benjamin. "On the Interpretation of Scripture." In *Essays and Reviews*, ed. J. Parker. London: Longman, 1860.

Käsemann, Ernst. "Is the Gospel Objective?" In *Essays on New Testament Themes*, trans. W. J. Montague, 48-62. Studies in Biblical Theology 41. London: SCM Press, 1964. Original: "Zum Thema der Nichtobjektivierbarkeit." *Evangelische Theologie* 12 (1952/1953): 455-66.

—————. "Sentences of Holy Law in the New Testament." In *New Testament Questions of Today*, trans. W. J. Montague and Wilfred F. Bunge, 66-81. London: SCM Press; Philadelphia: Fortress Press, 1969. Original: "Sätze Heiligen Rechtes im Neuen Testament." *New Testament Studies* 1 (1954/1955): 248-60.

Keating, Henry Raymond Fitzwalter. "The Five Senses of Mrs. Craggs." In *Ellery Queen's Murdercade*, 238-61. New York: Random House, 1975.

Knox, John. *The Church and the Reality of Christ*. New York and Evanston: Harper & Row, 1962; London: Collins, 1963.

Kümmel, Werner Georg. *The New Testament: The History of the Investigation of Its Problems*. Trans. S. McLean Gilmour and Howard C. Kee. London: SCM Press; Nashville/New York: Abingdon Press, 1972.

Kysar, Robert. "The Background of the Prologue of the Fourth Gospel: A Critique of Historical Methods." *Canadian Journal of Theology* 16 (1970): 250-55.

Lewis, Clive Staples. "Bulverism, or The Foundation of Twentieth-Century Thought." In *First and Second Things*, 13-18. London: Collins, 1985. Original: *Time and Tide* 22 (29 March 1941): 261.

—————. *Christian Reflections*. London: Collins, 1981. (London: Geoffrey Bles, 1967—different pagination.)

—————. "On the Reading of Old Books." In *First and Second Things*. London: Collins, 1985. (Originally published as introduction to a translation of Athanasius's *The Incarnation of the Word of God.*)

—————. *The Screwtape Letters*. London: Geoffrey Bles, 1942; London: Collins/Fontana Books, 1955.

Lonergan, Bernard Joseph Francis. *Method in Theology*. London: Darton, Longman & Todd; New York: Herder and Herder, 1972.

Lowell, James Russell. "The Present Crisis" (1845) as excerpted in the *Methodist Hymn Book*, hymn 898. London: Methodist Conference Office, 1933.

McArthur, Harvey K. "Computer Criticism." *Expository Times* 76 (1964/1965): 367-70.

McFague, Sallie. *See* TeSelle, Sallie McFague.

McWhirter, Norris, ed. *The Guinness Book of Records*. 1980 edition. Enfield: Guinness Superlatives Ltd., 1980.

Manson, Thomas Walter. *The Sayings of Jesus as Recorded in the Gospels according to St. Matthew and St. Luke*. London: SCM Press, 1949; Grand Rapids MI: Eerdmans,

1979. First published as part 2 of *The Mission and Message of Jesus: An Exposition of the Gospels in the Light of Modern Research*, ed. H. D. A. Major, 299-639. London: Nicholson & Watson, 1937; New York: E. P. Dutton, 1938.

Metzger, Bruce Manning. *The Text of the New Testament: Its Transmission, Corruption, and Restoration.* Oxford: Oxford University Press, 1964 (^{2}1968).

Mitton, Charles Leslie. "Vincent Taylor: New Testament Scholar." Introduction to *New Testament Essays by Vincent Taylor*, 5-30. London: Epworth Press, 1970.

Momigliano, Arnaldo. "The Historians of the Classical World and Their Audiences: Some Suggestions." Chapter 25 of *Sesto Contributo alla Storia degli Studi Classici e del Mondo Antico*, Tomo Primo, 361-76. Rome: Edizioni di Storia e Letteratura, 1980.

Morgan, Bryan, ed. *Crime on the Lines.* London: Routledge & Kegan Paul, 1975.

Morgan, Chris, and David Langford. *Facts and Fallacies.* Exeter: Webb and Bower, 1981.

Morton, Andrew Q., and James McLeman. *Christianity and the Computer.* London: Hodder & Stoughton, 1964.

Muir, Frank, and Denis Norden. *Upon My Word.* London: Eyre, Methuen, 1974.

Neill, Stephen Charles. *A History of Christian Missions.* Harmondsworth: Penguin Books; Baltimore: Penguin Books Inc., 1964.

_____. *The Interpretation of the New Testament 1861-1961.* Firth Lectures 1962. Corrected edition. London, New York, and Toronto: Oxford University Press, 1966 (^{1}1964).

Nineham, Dennis Eric. "Et hoc genus omne." In *Christian History and Interpretation: Studies Presented to John Knox*, ed. William R. Farmer, Charles F. D. Moule, and Richard R. Niebuhr, 199-222. Cambridge: Cambridge University Press, 1967.

_____. *The Gospel of Saint Mark.* Pelican Gospel Commentaries. Harmondsworth and Baltimore: Penguin Books, 1963. New York: Seabury Press, 1968. Also: *St. Mark.* Westminster Pelican Commentaries. Philadelphia: Westminster Press, 1978.

_____. *The Use and Abuse of the Bible.* London: Macmillan; New York: Barnes and Noble Books, 1976.

Packard, Vance. *The Hidden Persuaders.* London: Penguin Books, 1960.

Palmer, Humphrey. *The Logic of Gospel Criticism: An Account of the Methods and Arguments Used by Textual, Documentary, Source, and Form Critics of the New Testament.* London: Macmillan; New York: St. Martin's Press, 1968.

Panikkar, Raymond. "The Relation of the Gospels to Hindu Culture and Religion." In *Jesus and Man's Hope*, Pittsburgh Festival on the Gospels 1970, vol. 2 (Perspective 2), ed. Donald G. Miller and Dikran Y. Hadidian, 249-61. Pittsburgh: Pittsburgh Theological Seminary, 1971.

Perrin, Norman. *Rediscovering the Teaching of Jesus.* London: SCM Press; New York: Harper & Row, 1967.

Pile, Stephen. *The Book of Heroic Failures.* London: Futura Publications, 1980. (London: Routledge & Kegan Paul, 1979.)

Plumb, John Harold. *The Death of the Past.* London: Macmillan, 1969; Boston: Houghton Mifflin, 1970.

Poe, Edgar Allan. "The Murders in the Rue Morgue." In *The Complete Tales and Poems of Edgar Allan Poe*, 141-68. New York: The Modern Library, 1938.

Polybius. *The Rise of the Roman Empire*. Trans. Ian Scott-Kilvert. New York: Viking Penguin Inc.; London: Penguin Books, 1979.

Popper, Karl Raimund. *Unended Quest*. London: Collins, 1976. This is a revised edition of ''Autobiography of Karl Popper,'' in *The Philosophy of Karl Popper,* Library of Living Philosophers, ed. Paul Arthur Schlipp. Peru IL: Open Court Pub. Co., 1974.

Priestley, John Boynton. *Faraway*. London: Pan Books, 1967.

Pyke, Magnus. *There and Back*. London: John Murray, 1978.

Robinson, James McConkey. *A New Quest of the Historical Jesus*. Studies in Biblical Theology 25. London: SCM Press; Naperville IL: Alec R. Allenson, 1959. Missoula MT: Scholars Press, 1979.

Robinson, John Arthur Thomas. *Redating the New Testament*. London: SCM Press; Philadelphia: Westminster Press, 1976.

Rostovtzeff, Mikhail Ivanovich. *The Social and Economic History of the Roman Empire*. Oxford: Clarendon Press (Oxford University Press), 1926.

Rupp, Gordon. *Just Men*. London: Epworth Press, 1977.

Sanday, William. *The Life of Christ in Recent Research*. Oxford, New York: Oxford University Press, 1907. Louisville KY: Lost Cause Press, 1977.

Sayers, Dorothy Leigh. *Busman's Honeymoon*. London: Victor Gollancz, 1972.

_____. *The Man Born to Be King*. London: Victor Gollancz, 1943.

_____. *Unpopular Opinions*. London: Victor Gollancz, 1946.

Schumacher, Ernst Friedrich. *A Guide for the Perplexed*. London: Sphere Books, 1978. (Jonathan Cape, 1977.)

Schweitzer, Albert. *The Quest of the Historical Jesus: A Critical Study of Its Progress from Reimarus to Wrede*. Trans. W. Montgomery. Foreword by F. C. Burkitt. London: A & C Black, 1910. New York: Macmillan, 1961.

Dr. Seuss. *See* Geisel, Theodor Seuss.

Sider, Ronald A. ''The Historian, the Miraculous, and Post-Newtonian Man.'' *Scottish Journal of Theology 25 (1972): 309-19.*

Stein, Robert H. *An Introduction to the Parables of Jesus*. Philadelphia: Westminster Press, 1981.

Stonehouse, Ned Bernard. *Origins of the Synoptic Gospels: Some Basic Questions*. Grand Rapids MI: Eerdmans, 1963; London: Tyndale House, 1964.

Strecker, Georg. ''The Passion and Resurrection Predictions in Mark's Gospel.'' *Interpretation* 22 (1968): 440.

Streeter, Burnett Hillman, and Aiyadurai Jesudasen Appasamy. *The Sadhu*. London: Macmillan, 1921. USA: *The Message of Sadhu Sundar Singh*. New York: Macmillan, 1921.

Taylor, John Vernon. *The Primal Vision*. London: SCM Press; Philadelphia: Fortress Press, 1963.

Taylor, Vincent. ''The Alleged Neglect of M. Alfred Loisy.'' In *New Testament Essays,* 72-82. London: Epworth Press, 1970.

_____. ''The Creative Element in the Thought of Jesus.'' In *New Testament Essays,* 36-47. London: Epworth Press, 1970.

TeSelle, Sallie McFague. *Speaking in Parables: A Study in Metaphor and Theology*. Philadelphia: Fortress Press, 1975.

Thucydides. *The History of the Peloponnesian War*. Trans. Richard Crawley. London: J. M. Dent, 1903.

Toulmin, Stephen Edelston, and June Goodfield. *The Fabric of the Heavens*. London: Hutchinson, 1961; New York: Harper, 1962.

Trevor-Roper, Hugh R. Review of Walter Laqueur, *The Terrible Secret* (London: Weidenfeld, 1980). *The Listener* (1 January 1981): 19.

Via, Dan Otto, Jr. *The Parables*. Philadelphia: Fortress Press, 1967.

_____. *Kerygma and Comedy in the New Testament*. Philadelphia: Fortress Press, 1975.

Wijngaards, John N. M. "The Awe-inspiring Reality of Christ's Silence." *Indian Journal of Theology* 24 (1975): 132-42.

Wilder, Amos Niven. *Early Christian Rhetoric: The Language of the Gospel*. London: SCM Press, 1964. U.S.A.: *The Language of the Gospel: Early Christian Rhetoric*. New York: Harper & Row, 1964.

Wodehouse, Pelham Grenville. *Big Money*. London: Herbert Jenkins, 1931.

_____. *The Heart of a Goof*. London: Herbert Jenkins, 1926.

_____. *Performing Flea*. Harmondsworth: Penguin Books, 1961. (London: Herbert Jenkins, 1953.)

_____. *The Small Bachelor*. London: Methuen, 1933, 1927.

Wood, Herbert George. *Jesus in the Twentieth Century*. London: Lutterworth Press, 1960.

Wouk, Herman. *This Is My God*. London: Collins, 1976.

Wrede, William. *The Messianic Secret in the Gospels*. Trans. J. C. G. Greig. Cambridge: James Clarke, 1971. Library of Theological Translations. Greenwood SC: Attic Press, 1971.

Yule, George Udny. *The Statistical Study of Literary Vocabulary*. Cambridge: Cambridge University Press, 1944.

Index of Names and Subjects

Magic, Myth, and Mystery

ZOMBIES

DO YOU BELIEVE?

This series features creatures that excite our minds. They're magical. They're mythical. They're mysterious. They're also not real. They live in our stories. They're brought to life by our imaginations. Facts about these creatures are based on folklore, legends, and beliefs. We have a rich history of believing in the impossible. But these creatures only live in fantasies and dreams. Monsters do not live under our beds. They live in our heads!

45th Parallel Press

Published in the United States of America by Cherry Lake Publishing
Ann Arbor, Michigan
www.cherrylakepublishing.com

Reading Adviser: Marla Conn MS, Ed., Literacy specialist, Read-Ability, Inc.
Book Design: Felicia Macheske

45th Parallel Press is an imprint of Cherry Lake Publishing.

Library of Congress Cataloging-in-Publication Data

Names: Loh-Hagan, Virginia, author.
Title: Zombies : magic, myth, and mystery / by Virginia Loh-Hagan.
Description: Ann Arbor : Cherry Lake Publishing, [2016] | Series: Magic, myth, and mystery | Includes bibliographical references and index.
Identifiers: LCCN 2016004927| ISBN 9781634711111 (hardcover) | ISBN 9781634713092 (pbk.) | ISBN 9781634712101 (pdf) | ISBN 9781634714082 (ebook)
Subjects: LCSH: Zombies—Juvenile literature.
Classification: LCC GR581 .L64 2016 | DDC 398.21—dc23
LC record available at http://lccn.loc.gov/2016004927

Cherry Lake Publishing would like to acknowledge the work of The Partnership for 21st Century Skills.
Please visit www.p21.org for more information.

Printed in the United States of America
Corporate Graphics Inc.

TABLE of CONTENTS

Brain Eaters

What are zombies like? What are some types of zombies?

"Brains. Brains. Must eat brains." Zombies eat brains. They **infect** others. Infect means to spread sickness. They turn humans into zombies. More zombies mean a zombie **apocalypse**. This is when zombies take over. Zombies attack humans.

Zombies are **undead** creatures. Zombies are dead. But they act alive. They don't have free will. They can't think. They lost their former lives. They wear the clothes they died in.

Other undead creatures include mummies, ghosts, and vampires.

Explained by Science!

There are several diseases that cause zombie-like behaviors. A fly bite can cause sleeping sickness. The infection attacks the brain. Victims can't talk. They can't focus. They can't function. They can't move well. They can't sleep. They can become aggressive. Dysarthia affects the part of the brain that controls speech. It's caused by brain damage. Victims can't control their voice muscles. They moan and mumble. They sound like zombies. Necrosis attacks cells. Skin rots off. Victims look like zombies. Their bodies and brains shut down. Yaws is another disease. It infects skin, bones, and joints. It causes painful, oozing sores. Sores occur on faces, legs, arms, and feet. The sores on feet bottoms cause victims to shuffle slowly. Victims walk like zombies.

Zombies have **decomposing** bodies. Their bodies break down. Their skin slowly rots. Their flesh falls off. Their muscles are damaged. They smell really bad.

Zombies limp. They move slowly. They're clumsy. They walk in a zigzag. They hang their heads. They moan. They groan.

Zombies' brains don't work. They're not smart. But they're focused. They destroy. They eat. Nothing stops them.

There's no such thing as a solitary zombie. Where there's one, there's more.

There are different types of zombies. Walkers are the most common. They're regular zombies.

Runner zombies are the most dangerous. They can run. They're fast. They're new zombies. They still have some human strength.

Crawlers don't have legs. Their lower bodies were chopped off. They crawl. They bite ankles.

Spitters spit poison. Their spit burns. It infects. They can spit far.

Bonies are what zombies become. Their flesh has completely rotted off. They have no eyes. They're old zombies.

All types of zombies are dangerous.

Chapter Two

Beware of Zombies!

How are zombies stronger than humans? How do zombies eat?

Zombies are scary. They're dead. But they still move. They bite. They attack. They eat humans.

They're most powerful when first infected. They still have their body parts. They can still move like humans.

They're stronger than humans. They never get tired. They never sleep. They don't feel pain. They live without regular food or water.

They don't need air. They don't breathe. They can live on land. They can live under water. They can't drown.

Zombies aren't hurt by drugs, poisons, gases, electricity, or suffocation.

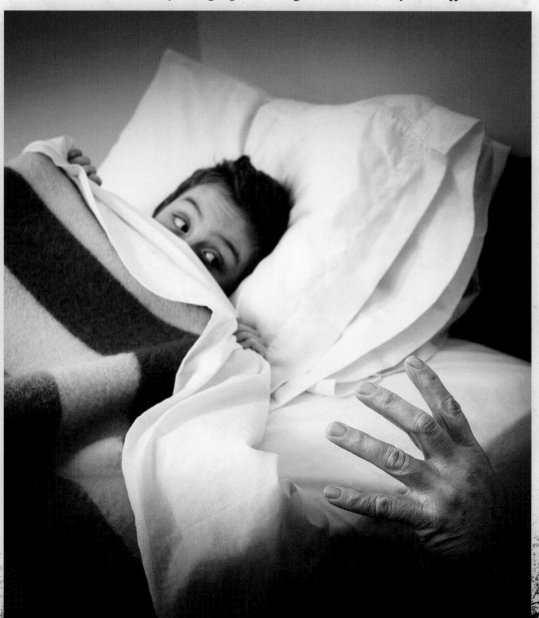

Zombies can hear well. They can smell well. They use these skills to attack.

They like noise. They go to the noise. They attack in **hordes**. Hordes are zombie groups. But zombies don't act like a team. They act separately. They just happen to be doing the same thing.

Their strength is in numbers. They overcome humans. They attack from all sides. They wait for humans to fall. They trap humans. Then they eat. Humans are their food.

Zombies travel in packs.

When Fantasy Meets Reality!

Jewel wasps sting cockroaches. They inject poison. They paralyze the cockroaches' front legs. Paralyze means to not be able to move. Cockroaches can't escape. Jewel wasps sting again. They slide their stingers into the cockroaches' heads. They poke at the brains. They find the right spot. They inject poison. They control the cockroaches' brains. The cockroaches become like zombies. Jewel wasps chew off half the cockroaches' feelers. They drag them to their homes. They lay white eggs on the cockroaches' stomachs. The baby wasps feed on the cockroaches. They chew into the cockroaches' stomachs. They chew on the organs. Then they burst through the cockroaches. That's how jewel wasps are born.

Zombies tend to hang out where they used to live.

Stronger zombies eat first. They eat brains. They eat organs. They leave the bones. Weaker zombies break open the bones. They eat the stuff inside bones.

Feeding time can be dangerous. Zombies damage each other. They push. They shove. They grab. They pull apart body parts. They don't share food.

Zombies find places with lots of humans. They like hospitals. They like malls. They like churches. These are "hot spots." Zombies prefer cities. They want to be close to food.

Chapter Three

Zombie Weaknesses

**What are some ways to kill zombies?
What are some zombie weaknesses?**

Most zombies are slower than humans. They can't move well. They're not flexible. They can't use tools. They can't open doors. They can't use stairs. It's easy to kill one zombie. But it's hard to kill a horde.

There are several ways to kill zombies. First, damage their brains. Second, cut off their heads. Third, set them on fire. Fires kill zombies. But zombies won't feel the fires. They'll stumble around. They'll spread the fire.

Fire isn't the best weapon. Swords work better.
Quiet weapons are best. Noise draws more zombies.

Zombies don't have superpowers.
They have fewer abilities than when they were humans.

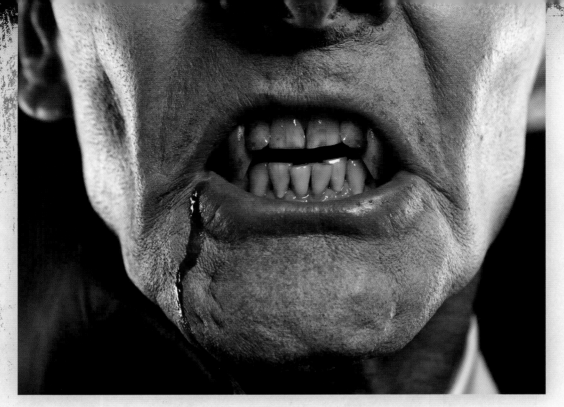

In a fight against vampires, zombies would lose.

Zombies can't see well. They can't see at night. They use other senses.

They can't heal. They can't grow. Sometimes, they lose body parts. Nothing can be done about that.

They don't have many moves. They can't swim. They can't fly. They can only shuffle.

Zombies rot away. They get weaker. They go from walking to crawling. Eventually, they won't move at all.

SURVIVAL TIPS!

- Go to Australia. It's the safest area. Canada is second. The United States is third. These areas were rated based on location, land features, military and weapon access, and population size.

- Feed salt to a zombie. This will make the zombies return to the grave.

- Get fit. Build running skills. Do weight training. Learn martial arts.

- Don't hide in a car unless you have keys. Avoid getting trapped in small spaces.

- Get enough food and water to last 14 to 90 days.

- Stand against a wall. Or stand back-to-back with someone. Make sure no zombies can come behind you.

- Don't use weapons that take time to use. This gives zombies time to bite you.

Chapter Four

Becoming a Zombie

How do people become zombies?

There are several ways to become a zombie. A person dies. Then the person becomes undead. The person becomes a zombie. This process doesn't take long.

A person can get **cursed**. A curse is a magic spell. The curse makes the person undead. These zombies are magical.

A person can get bitten by a zombie. Bites pass

the sickness. The sickness spreads from the zombie to the person.

There is no cure. Once a person is bitten, that person is doomed.

A person can get poisoned. This happens from **radiation**. Energy bursts from a source. The source is usually a bomb. It's also power plant explosions. Radiation attacks anything in its reach.

A person can get a **parasite**. A parasite lives on a **host**. A host can be a person. A common parasite is a worm. The worm attacks the host. It turns a person into a zombie.

Zombie infections can't jump **species**. Species are groups of living things. Humans can't infect animals. Animals can't infect humans.

Dormant infection means that everyone has the potential to be a zombie.

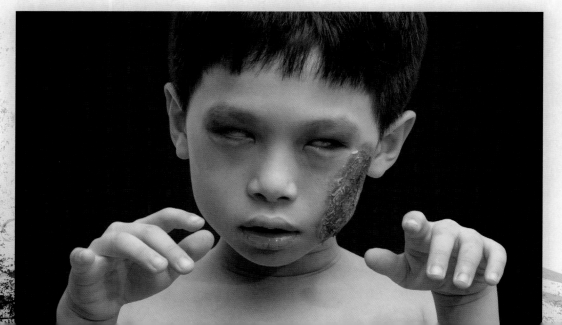

Know the Lingo!

- **Ankle biters:** zombies that don't have legs; also known as crawlers or draggers

- **Chewscrew:** a deep zombie bite that goes into muscle

- **Cluster:** a group of zombies in a small confined area

- **Drone:** the sound a horde makes that can be heard from a distance

- **Grabbers:** zombies trapped inside abandoned cars who reach out of windows to grab victims

- **Grab zone:** the area around a zombie in which a victim can be grabbed

- **Lurkers:** zombies that pretend to be dead; they hide and wait for victims to come close, and then attack

- **Noob:** newly infected zombie

- **RLF:** "reanimated life-form," another word for zombie

- **Swimmers:** bloated and waterlogged zombies, also known as floaters

- **Walkers:** another term for zombies; refers to walking dead

- **ZCORE:** Zombie Coalition Offensive Response Elite, a professional zombie survival group

- **Zombophiles:** fans of zombie films and books

Chapter Five

History of Zombies

How did the word zombie develop? How are zombies featured in different cultures?

Zombie stories started in West Africa. It started with **voodoo**. Voodoo is a religion. It uses folk magic.

Zombie is a special word. It comes from different sources. *Nzambi* is a West African word. It means "spirit of a dead person." It also means "god."

Slaves were brought to America from West Africa. They were sent to Haiti. Haiti is a Caribbean island. Their word for zombie is *jumbie*. It means "ghost."

Slaves also traveled to Louisiana. Their word is

zonbi. This means a person who died and came back.

William Seabrook wrote *The Magic Island*. He wrote it in 1929. He described his time in Haiti. He described a dead man coming back to life. He created the term *zombie*.

Zombies started with the Yoruba tribe in West Africa.

Real-World Connection

There was a zombie-like attack in China. A male bus driver was driving. His name is Dong. A woman driver pulled in front of him. Her name is Du. She blocked his path. He got mad. He jumped on top of her car. He hit the car. She stepped out of her car. She screamed for help. The man jumped on her. He wrestled her to the ground. He bit her face. Du was covered in blood. People tried to pull Dong off her. Police grabbed Dong. Du survived. But she needed surgery to fix her nose and lips. Some believed *jiangshi* took over Dong's body.

Haitians prevent zombies.
They bury bodies under heavy stones.
They watch over the grave for 36 hours.
They cut the heads off.

In Haiti, zombies are created by **bokors**. Bokors are evil priests. They made special drugs. These drugs made people look dead.

Clairvius Narcisse thought he was a zombie slave. He ate the special drugs. He looked dead. He was buried. But he was still alive. He was taken from the grave. He was forced to work on a farm. He worked for several years. Then the owner died. Narcisse returned to his family. People investigated. They found out Narcisse's brother drugged him and sold him to the farm owner. They were fighting over land. His brother wanted to get rid of him.

There are zombies in Chinese stories. Chinese zombies are called *jiangshi*. That means "hopping **corpse**." Corpse is a dead body. They died far from home. They can't rest in peace. They want to get back home. They take energy from humans.

There are zombies in Scandinavian stories. They're called *draugr*. They were fighters. They died. They came back to life. They attack humans.

Long ago, some people were buried alive. Doctors thought they were dead. But they weren't. Thieves dug up their graves. They wanted to steal jewelry. But they got a surprise. The people in the graves were still alive! The thieves thought the dead had risen. These stories made zombies a part of our culture.

Zombie stories have been found in Europe, Asia, North America, Africa, and the Middle East.

Did You Know?

- October 8 is World Zombie Day. Many cities celebrate. People dress as zombies. They walk in a parade.

- Mummies are undead. But they're not zombies. Zombies are always decaying. Mummies are preserved. They're saved from decaying as quickly.

- The Centers for Disease Control and Prevention (CDC) wants people to be prepared. It wants people to survive disasters. It created a plan for zombies. It said, "If zombies did start roaming the streets, CDC would conduct an investigation much like any other disease outbreak."

- George Washington was almost the first "zombie president" of the United States. He died in 1799. His dead body was on ice for three days. William Thornton wanted to bring Washington back to life. He wanted to pump air into Washington's lungs. He wanted to give Washington lamb's blood. Washington's family said no.

- Zombies last longest in cold weather. The cold and snow preserve their bodies.

- There's a zombie law in Haiti. It's a crime to turn people into zombies.

- The 1932 film *White Zombie* was the first appearance of a zombie.

- Zombies are mentioned in *Epic of Gilgamesh*. This story is over 5,000 years old. It features an angry goddess. The goddess threatens to bring the dead back to eat the living.

Consider This!

Take a Position: Read about other undead creatures. (45th Parallel Press has a book about vampires.) Where do you rank zombies in regard to other undead creatures? Which undead creature is the scariest? Argue your point with reasons and evidence.

Say What? What would you do in a zombie apocalypse? Explain your fears. Explain your survival strategies.

Think About It! Dr. Frankenstein's monster is famous. It's made up of dead bodies. It was brought back to life. But is it a zombie? Many zombie fans don't think so. Learn more about Frankenstein's monster. (The book was written by Mary Wollstonecraft Shelley.) Then, decide for yourself.

Learn More

- Hamilton, S. L. *Zombies*. Edina, MN: ABDO Publishing, 2011.

- Jenson-Elliot, Cindy. *Zombies*. San Diego: KidHaven Press, 2006.

- Owen, Ruth. *Zombies and Other Walking Dead*. New York: Bearport Publishing, 2013.

Glossary

apocalypse (uh-POK-uh-lips) the final destruction of the civilized world

bokors (BO-kurz) evil priests in Haiti

corpse (KORPS) a dead body

cursed (KURSD) put under a magical spell

decomposing (dee-kuhm-POHZ-ing) decaying or rotting in the process of dying

hordes (HORDZ) groups of zombies

host (HOHST) a person or the thing providing life to a parasite

infect (in-FEKT) to contaminate, to spread sickness

parasite (PAR-uh-site) a thing living off of a host

radiation (ray-dee-AY-shuhn) energy bursting from a source and spreading poison

species (SPEE-sheez) groups of living things

undead (un-DED) dead but brought back to life

voodoo (VOO-doo) a religion that started in West Africa

Index

About the Author

Dr. Virginia Loh-Hagan is an author, university professor, former classroom teacher, and curriculum designer. She feels like a zombie every morning. She's a big fan of *The Walking Dead*. She lives in San Diego with her very tall husband and very naughty dogs. To learn more about her, visit www.virginialoh.com.

I'll Never Love Anything Ever Again

Judy Delton
pictures by Rodney Pate

Albert Whitman & Company, Niles, Illinois

Library of Congress Cataloging in Publication Data

Delton, Judy.
  I'll never love anything ever again.

  Summary: A little boy's allergies force him to give
away his beloved dog.
  1. Children's stories, American. [1. Allergy—Fiction.
2. Dogs—Fiction]   I. Pate, Rodney, 1939—ill.   II. Title.
PZ7.D388Il 1985   [E]   84-17271
ISBN 0-8075-3521-4 (lib. bdg.)

For Margi Mark,
who hates dogs but loves books
and is one of the most talented writers I know.

I've had my dog, Tinsel, all my life. Since I was born.
Now the doctor says he has to leave.

He says I've become allergic to Tinsel.
The allergies make my eyes water and my throat sore.
They cause infections, and then I run a fever.

How could something I love so much make me sick?

My mom says the doctor is right. She says
she will try to find a new home for Tinsel
before I miss any more school.

He can't leave! He's family.

I've got pictures of Tinsel when he was a baby. See, here he is with me when I was almost as little as he was. His hair is all curly, and his face, look! He's smiling at me.

When I was four, we went to the city and left him in a
kennel. When we picked him up, the man said Tinsel
wouldn't eat, he was so lonely. But when we got home,
he gobbled up everything in sight. Even the generic
dog food he hates.

When he leaves us, he'll probably starve to death.

Tinsel plays tug-of-war with me. He pulls and pulls on his blue ring. He growls and arches his back and digs his heels in the ground, but in the end, he always lets me win.

I don't know any other dog that would let someone else win, on purpose.

When we walk to the store together, I tie him to the mailbox. He doesn't move till I come out. Then his tail wags so hard that it beats like a drum on the sides of the mailbox.

Now I suppose he'll wait for someone else. He'll probably forget all about me in a couple of weeks. Or maybe he won't, and he'll die of homesickness.

When we ride in the car, he never takes his eyes off the road. I think that's unusual for a dog. Most dogs I know sleep in the car. Not Tinsel. He drives all the way.

The new owner won't know Tinsel loves to drive. And he won't know that Tinsel doesn't like turn signals. My mom goes out of her way so she doesn't have to turn corners. The new owner will probably use signals all the time. It will drive Tinsel crazy.

I never knew how much I loved Tinsel, until now. I didn't know it could feel this bad to love something. I'll never get another pet, even if the doctor says it's okay.

If one person sets foot on our lawn, Tinsel barks. When the meter man comes, we have to lock Tinsel up. Even my friends can't get in until Tinsel sniffs them.

Yes, he is some watchdog.

Who will guard our house now?

At night when I'm doing my homework, he sneaks up and puts his chin on my lap. I rub his neck even if I'm busy, because he likes attention. He hates to be ignored.

If I hug my mom, he comes up and puts his head between us, because he's jealous.

I don't think the new owner will have time to give Tinsel all the attention he needs.

Tinsel's ears are so soft and silky, I put my face in them and hug him. Who will I hug that way now? Tinsel was always there. And now he won't be.

I won't let them take him!

My mom is getting together his things—his blue ring and his ball with the bell in it that he can catch in the air and his red dish that he eats out of. I want to unpack them and yell "STOP! No one else can have my dog! He loves ME, not someone he doesn't even know —someone who doesn't know where he likes to run in the park and that he only shakes hands with his left paw and that when you say 'heel,' he sits up. No one knows all about Tinsel but me."

I run to my room and cry. I don't care if I have allergies! I don't care if I miss school! I don't care if I die! No one else is getting my dog!

My mom comes in and sits on my bed.

"He's too big to give away!" I say. "Give away my goldfish or my turtle. Don't give my Tinsel away."

"You aren't allergic to your goldfish or turtle," she says sensibly. I hate it when my mom is sensible.

"I'm never going to love anything, ever again," I say.

"Yes, you will," says my mother, rubbing my hair. She doesn't look too happy herself. I think she hates to see Tinsel go, too.

"I will not," I yell. "Never, never!"

Then she says, "Think of all the happy times with Tinsel. You wouldn't have had them if you didn't love him."

"It's the happy times that make me feel sad," I say. "They make me feel awful."

"Remember when Grandpa died?" my mom says. "You thought you'd never feel better and then later you said how good it was to remember the things you'd done together. Before long you will remember the happy times with Tinsel without feeling sad."

"I doubt it," I say.

"Give it time," says my mother.

When I come home from school the next day, my mom is waiting at the door. "Guess what?" she says in an excited voice. "Mrs. Matson's son Bud wants to take Tinsel!"

Mrs. Matson is our neighbor. She used to babysit for me when I was little.

"He loves animals," my mom goes on, "and he lives on a farm, where Tinsel can run loose. There's even a lake, so Tinsel can swim. You know how Tinsel likes to swim."

I feel a little better, but not much, knowing where Tinsel is going to live.

"Bud says you can come and stay in the summer, for a visit, and play with him."

I don't want to *visit* Tinsel. I want him to be my dog!

Still, I've never been in the country to stay. It might be
fun to see a real farm. And Tinsel does like to run and
swim. My mom is right about that.

Tinsel leaves today. Mrs. Matson's son is here to get him. He brings Tinsel one of those rawhide bones. Tinsel just sniffs it. He doesn't take bones from strangers.

"I'll bet it's hard to give up your dog," Bud Matson says to me. "When I was your age I had a dog. Then we moved to an apartment and had to get rid of him. It was awful."

"I'll be okay," I say. I don't want help from this guy.

"It means a lot to me to have a dog again."

I don't answer. Tinsel sniffs the bone. He picks it up and brings it to me. I throw it into the car. Tinsel jumps in after it. He thinks I am coming, too.

"See you in June," says Mrs. Matson's son, starting the car. Tinsel looks out the back window at me as they drive off. I feel like a traitor or something.

"I'll come!" I call to him, with tears in my eyes. "I'll
come in June, Tinsel."

My mom is crying now, too. I bet she'll miss Tinsel
almost as much as I will.

"It's not very long till June, you know," she says.

June seems years away to me. I don't think I'll ever love anything ever again. At least not for a long, long time.